V Kratinově „První Modní Akademii"

počíná každé pondělí neb 1. a 15. v měsíci nový střihačský kurs k vyučování kreslení dámských střihů, braní míry atd.

 V Akademii vyučuje se všem **nejmodernějším** střihům dle nové vyučovací soustavy centimetrové. — Kratinova Akademie získala právě nejnovější tvary všech módních střihů ze světových akademií, s nimiž jest ve stálém spojení. — Akademie tato byla povolena velesl. c. k. místodržitelstvím v Praze r. 1894 a jest prvním a nejoblíbenějším ústavem toho druhu v království Českém. — Zvláštní atelier ku zhotovování veškerých dámských módních střihů. — Prospekty zdarma a franko zasílá

„První Modní Akademie" v Praze I., Melantrichova 15. ◨ Majitel JAN KRATINA.

V Kratinově „První Modní Akademii" v Praze

lze mimo tohoto časopisu ještě násl. dámské módní listy obdržeti:

„Dámské Módní Listy". Časopis elegantních toalet. Vycházejí v těchto měsících: V lednu, březnu, dubnu, květnu, červenci, září, říjnu a listopadu. Předplatné na celý rok K 12·—. V eleganci a praktičnosti dosud žádným módním žurnálem nedostižen. **Celoroční předplatitelé obdrží čtyři nádherná bluzová alba úplně zdarma.**

„Album kostýmů a plášťů" pro období jarní a letní 1915 — jež obsahuje vyobrazení různých nejelegantnějších druhů žaketů, plášťů a anglických úborů. Cena K 3·50.

Vkusně provedené **„Bluzové Album"** s mnoha vyobraz. pro období jarní a letní 1915. Cena K 1·50.

Praktický módní časopis (Modenschau). (Vychází 10krát ročně.) :: Předplatné: na celý rok K 8·—. Celoroční předplatitelé obdrží jako premii krásné bluzové album úplně **zdarma**.

Velké módní album pod názvem

„MODEALBUM"

obsahující v nejelegantnějším provedení **1000 vyobrazení dámských úborů**, jako: Moderních kostýmů, žaketů, plášťů, sukní, bluz, různých obleků vycházkových, salonních, plesových a smutečních, obleků dětských a vůbec veškerých novinek **pro rok 1915**.

Cena K 2·50. Pro odběratele těchto listů K 2·—.

Kratinovy Módní Listy a střihy jsou, jak všeobecně uznáno, nejlepší.

Kupujte pouze kapesní kinematograf **Lux**, 1 obrázkové serie **Lux**, neboť jen tehdy je plně zaručena prvotřídní optika a bezvadné sestavení serií.

Apartní kloboučky, které každé dámě sluší, **RŮŽA PTÁČKOVÁ.** PRAHA II., Školská 14. Apartní kloboučky od 9 K výše. Opravy za 2 K jako nové.

 **Božena Socháňová,** Sklad ručních výšivek slovenských. Zhotovuje moderní šaty krojové dle míry. Prodává slovácké halenky, výbavy, soupravy pokojové, různé přikrývky. Národní kroje původní i půjčuje. Praha-Nusle, Vladimírova ul. č. 567, nároží Havlíčkovy třídy, konečná stanice elektr. trati č. 3

Strana 19.

136a.—137a. Zadní pohledy k vyobr. 136—137.

142. Klobouček s moderním závojem.

Máte dobrý střih?

92 cm

142a. Přehled střihu závoje k vyobr. 142.

Obraťte se s důvěrou na "První Modní Akademii" v Praze.

138a.—139a. Zadní pohledy k vyobr. 138—139.

136. Halenka z hedvábí. Střih XX. na střih. příl.

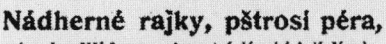

Sněrovačky
nejnovějších pařížských a vídeňských tvarů doporučuje ve velkém výběru jediná nejstarší česká firma
Julie Tesařová,
Praha-II., Ferdinandova třída číslo 61
Též na venek zásilky k výběru

Nádherné rajky, pštrosí péra,
nejmodernější formy, elegantní dámské i dívčí zdobené klobouky, jakož i veškeré přípravy pro P. T. modistky, skutečně nejlevněji nakoupíte u fy
BOŽENA KEMROVÁ, Král. Vinohrady, Karlova tř. 15.
Stanice el. dr. č. 2 a 3. — Modistkám zvláštní výhody.

Pensionát pro dívky.
Obecná a měšťanská škola s právem veřejnosti, hospodyňská a pokračovací škola.
Izabela Tschakertová, Praha
dříve pensionát J. Kirschbaumové. Založen r. 1855.
Vodičkova ul. 28.

Č. 41. Monogram.

Č. 39. Batistový noční čepec.
Střih a vysvětl. na zadní str.
příl. stř. č. XXIII, fig. 73 a 74.

Č. 37. Noční kazajka pro ženské.
Střih a vysvětl. na zadní str. příl. stř.

Č. 35. Košile, jež se na ramenou zapíná.
Střih a vysvětl. na zadní str. příl. stř. č. XX, fig. 66—69.

Č. 34. Střih a

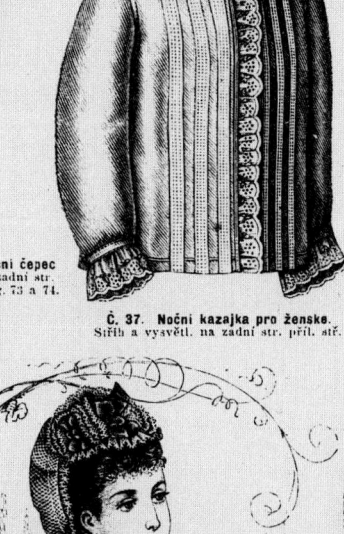

Č. 51. Košile mužská.
Střih a vysvětl. na zadní str. příl. stř. č. XVII, fig. 54—66.

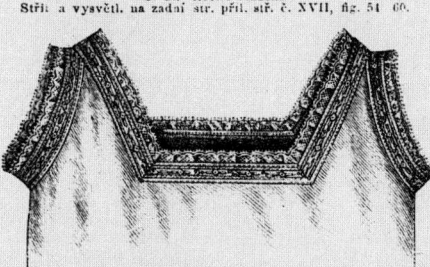

Č. 43. Límeček pro pány. Střih a vysvětl. na přední str. příl. stř. č. XII, fig. 37 a 38.

Č. 45. Ženská košile noční.
Střih a vysvětl. na zadní str. příl. stř. č. XV, fig. 45—48.

Č. 49. Vzoreček k bílému vyšívání.

Č. 53. Čepeček síťkovaný, fiší z mulu a krajek.

Č. 55. Košile s vložkou a krajkami.
Střih a vysvětl. na zadní příl. stř. č. XXI, fig. 70.

Č. 59. Příúčesný plášť, zdobený vložkou a krajkami.
Vysvětl. na zadní str. příl. stř.

Č. 61 a 62. Batistový župan.
Pohled na přední i zadní stranu.
Vysvětl. na zadní str. příl. stř.

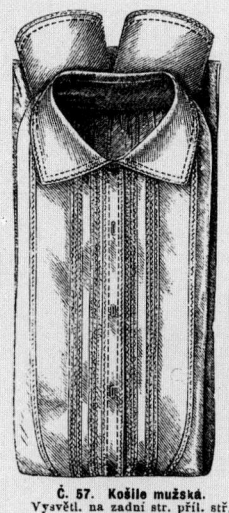

Č. 57. Košile mužská.
Vysvětl. na zadní str. příl. stř.

Č. 70. Šírtinkové spodky pro dámy.
Střih a vysvětl. na zadní str. příl. stř. č. XXII, fig. 71 a 72.

Č. 72. Vzoreček k bílému vyšívání.

Č. 68. Spodnička šírtinková, ozdobená vložkami a kraječkami.
Střih a vysvětl. na přední str. příl. stř.

Č. 65. Župan z mušelínu vlněného.

Eva Uchalová

CZECH FASHION
1870–1918
From the Waltz to the Tango

OLYMPIA

*publishing house in cooperation
with the Museum of Decorative Arts in Prague*

Deposits of the Museum of Decorative Arts were used in the publication.
© PhDr. Eva Uchalová, 1994, 1997
Photography © Miloslav Šebek, 1994, 1997
Translation © Capricorn Promotions
ISBN 80-7033-464-9

DĚTSKÉ OBLEKY.
(POPIS VIZ NA STR. 182.)

„PAŘÍŽSKÉ MODY" 1. KVĚTNA 1894.

NAKLADATEL JOS. R. VILÍMEK V PRAZE.

Introduction

Society

The apparel, with its forms depending on changes of fashion, and formal dance are sensitive forms of expression, which truly reflect the atmosphere of any historical period. The history of fashion and formal dance present our ancestors as real persons with their contemporary taste and vanity, reacting on various impulses that influenced their time. Nothing but the development of dancing balls representative of Czech society, called Národní beseda, which became active witnesses of the resurrection of the Czech nation, can better illustrate our reflections.[1/]

In the 1840's and the 1850's, when the character of balls had been established, dancing was combined with Czech literature programmes such as the reading of Czech poetry. This fact also determined the name of these balls - "talks" - which became standard in 1861. Those "beseda" were the first public meeting places for Czech society, which were conducted in Czech and henceforth the first public place where Czech became a language of the middle-class and Czech intellectuals. The character of the balls remained the same throughout the 1860's and was further emphasised by the dress of the ladies and gentleman. Ladies wore dresses in national colours, inspired by the national costume, with bodices and blouses, men wore strictly chamarres. Chamarres were not richly decorated, they were just black coats with simple cuts and were fastened with loops. In the intervals Czech poetry was read as well as congratulatory telegrams from patriots from Czech villages and towns. According to contemporary commentaries, the attendance of Czech historical aristocracy at this ball was high in 1868. This demonstrative attendance was apparently prompted by the anti-Czech attitude of Viennese government, which passed the law of Austro-Hungarian settlement in 1867 without taking Czech interests into account.

Contemporaries considered Národní beseda in 1870 to be a great and successful event as it raised an extraordinary sum of money for the building of the National Theatre. The atmosphere of Národní beseda in 1871, at the time of the Franco-Prussian war, showed sympathies towards the French. Clothes appeared with red and blue tunics and white mantle and Marseillaise was played. During the next years Národní beseda went through various crises as a results of disagreements between two contemporary political groups "Staročeši" and "Mladočeši" and also as a results of economic difficulties "although the present material conditions were extremely difficult, Národní Beseda still maintained its reputation as Prague's best ball" (1876).[2/]

Despite the continuous praise of ladies' toilettes, a reporter wished in 1880 to highlight even further the sense of pageantry in order to increase the success of Czech elegance in competition with German elegance. Ladies clothing in the 1870's and the 1880's followed the most modern fashion tendencies while in men's clothing chamarre competed with evening dress. In 1878 a reporter expressed his pleasure at the fact that most men wore chamarre but in 1881 he sadly admitted that "tail coat has somehow become our national dress."[3/] At the same time he claimed that during the whole decade chamarre worn in Národní beseda determined the fashion style for the year.

The step down from romantic patriotism was expressed not only by the style of dress but also by the absence of literary interludes and readings of congratulatory telegrams. This situation prompted these first reactions: "In Národní beseda, there appears every phase in the development of modern Czech society: hidden, but efficient patriotic work in the 1850's, patriotic enthusiasm with a hint of certain nice naivety in the 1860's, political struggle at the beginning of the 1870's, the split in 1876 and, to be perfectly honest, also a current blasé attitude, which prevails among us at the expense of our good intentions."[4/]

The importance of Národní beseda as an elite dancing ball representative of Czech society increased even further during the next few years. Among those, who regularly took part, there were not only members of the Czech aristocracy as patrons, members of the ball committee or dance leaders, but, starting in 1888, also official political guests, members of parliament, representatives of Czech industry, banking, culture, art and sometimes even members of the royal family, such as Archduke Ferdinand in 1889, and, starting in 1899, also foreign diplomats serving in Prague, whose presence expressed the acknowledgement of the Czech nation as an independent political subject.[5/]

Národní besedy were just a small part of the

rapidly developing social life of Czech society, which, thanks to its heterogeneity created new stimulation and work for fashion production. However, it should be noted, that Prague's society was Czech, Jewish and German during the whole of the period mentioned up until the Second World War and, therefore, although in this introduction we observe social life in Prague from a Czech point of view, we have to keep in mind that fashion production was an affair concerning the whole of Prague and therefore it was created by the cooperation of all three nationalities.

The building of the National Theatre became an event which raised the biggest ambitions and attracted the attention and efforts of the whole nation. The laying of the foundation stone on 16th May 1868 became a big national celebration, which was seen by thousands of people from all regions of Bohemia as well as by compatriots from abroad. The National Railway brought 25 thousand people on 14th May and another 24 special trains came the following day. The celebration began a regatta, with fireworks and light-pictures on the river Vltava in the evening. A festive parade took place the next day. It included representatives of the Czech and Moravian regions, Sokols from Prague and from 14 other associations, the committee for the construction of the National Theatre, members of the guilds in uniform, singing clubs and workers. The music was played by the Band of Prague Infantry. The celebration finished with a public banquet and entertainment on Letná hill.[6/]

Many years passed from the laying of the foundation stone of the National Theatre to its completion and therefore the opening proposed for 11th September 1881 should have been a reason for yet another national celebration. It was not, however, the theatre, opened ahead of schedule on 11th June 1881 because of the visit of prince Rudolf with his Belgian wife, princess Stefanie, was completely destroyed by fire on 12 August. The grief of the nation soon turned into unbelievable

Visitors
of the National Theatre.
Drawings of B. Roubalík,
after 1883.

Ballroom at Žofín.
Světozor 1870, p. 10.

Dance orde of the ball
of Academic Reader's Association.
Designed by R. Kremlička.
12 January 1909, inv. no. 16.470.

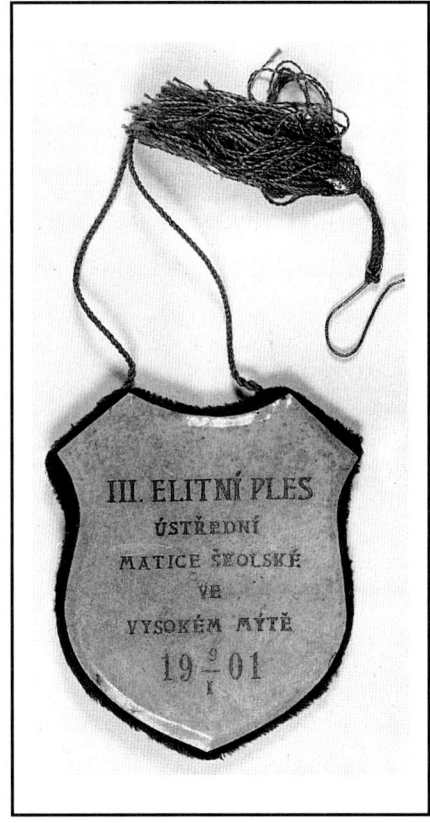

Dance order.
Vysoké Mýto 1901,
inv. no. 23.259/116.

Dance order.
19 January 1881,
inv. no. 71.429.

Dance order.
Around 1905,
inv. no. GS-15.950.

activity - the theatre was reconstructed in just two years' time and finally reopened on 18th November 1883.

Although the opening itself took place without any big national celebrations, the National Theatre became the centre of many national pilgrimages. During the next few years the "theatre trains" brought thousands of people from Bohemia and Moravia and also many compatriots from Vienna and Budapest. A special ship also brought compatriots from America.[7]

The new building and patriotic feelings were not the only reasons for attracting so many visitors to the National Theatre. The management of the theatre concentrated right from the beginning on an international repertoire and world-class singers such as the star of La Scala in Milan, Emma Turolla, who became so popular that crowds of people followed her every move in Prague. The bouquet of flowers she received after her last performance in the National Theatre, measured more than a metre in diameter and 4 metres in perimeter.[8] Turolla-mania could not escape the attention of Jan Neruda, who wrote ironically about the morning brawls of Prague ladies for tickets for the evening performance, which left pieces of lace, silk buttons, hair-pins and even the heel of a lady's shoe in front of the ticket office.[9] The orientation of the theatre towards an international repertoire meant a neglect of Czech works, amongst which were also the new operas of Bedřich Smetana. This was criticized by the public as well as by the experts. The situation changed after successful guest performances of the National Theatre at the International Fair of Music and Theatre in Vienna in 1893, which was the first of its kind. Czech music literally captivated the senses of the European public.[10]

Besides the National Theatre there were quite a few other old theatres as well as newly opened ones, above all the Nostic Theatre rebuilt in 1859, which in that period had only a German repertoire, and also the New German Theatre from 1886 - 1897 on the site of the New Town Theatre. The middle-class from Vinohrady built their own theatre between 1905 and 1907. In addition to these traditional scenes many theatres existed which were situated in provisional wooden arenas such as Pišťek's Arena in Vinohrady, arenas in Libeň and Holešovice, the National Arena and the New Czech Theatre, to name but a few.[11]

Amongst manifestations of national revival were also included celebrations of prominent Czech individuals. Their birthdays, anniversa-

Dance order of representative ball of the Academy of Commerce. Designed by F. Schenk. 16 April 1912, inv. no. GS-18.837.

ries, burials, the laying of foundation stones for their memorials and their unveiling became important social events. The laying of the foundation stone of the Josef Jungmann memorial in 1873 and its completion in 1878 were connected with large celebrations. The 500th anniversary of the death of Charles IV was commemorated with a solemn mass at the site of his memorial on Křižovnické square. The most honoured person of that period was undoubtedly František Palacký, "father of the nation". His 70th birthday was celebrated with a festive procession and banquet in Stromovka park. His burial in 1876 was attended by a crowd of 50 thousand people.[12/] The laying of the foundation stone of the Palacký memorial also became a national celebration in which thousands of people from all over Bohemia as well as representatives of other Slavic countries took part. The celebration peaked with the parade of allegorical triumphal carriage, which crossed the whole of Prague from Vinohrady to the present Palackého square.[13/]

The nation also gained monuments to its historical, political, economic and cultural successes by the creation of new representative buildings for cultural and economic purposes, which were designed in the style of historicism. The Rudolfinum, a centre for both music and graphic art together, was built between 1876 and 1882 at the expense of the Czech Savings Bank. Besides the concert hall there were unusually well-designed exhibition halls with an exhibition of paintings which belonged to the Society of Patriotic Friends of Art. There were also the first exhibits of the Museum of Deco-

Dance order of "Národní beseda" ball. Designed by Fr. Kysela. 21 January 1913, inv. no. GS-16.473.

Dance order of the ball of the Academic Reader's Association. Designed by R. Kremlička. 14 January 1908, inv. no. GS-16.649.

Dance order "Pohádka" for the ball of the School of Decorative Arts in Prague, 20 February 1914, inv. no. GS-13.044.

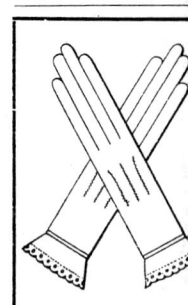

rative Arts. The museum was founded in 1885 by the Chamber of Trade and Commerce. However it did not obtain its own building until 1900. New buildings were also created for the National Museum, the Museum of Prague as well as all important economic institutions such as the Savings Bank and other banks, insurance companies and a number of schools.

Retrospective economic exhibitions became great events for Czech society.

Czech producers regularly took part in the World Exhibitions as part of the Austro-Hungarian Empire. However, the most important event in this field was the Anniversary Regional Exhibition, which took place in Prague in 1891 in the year of the 100th anniversary of the first Industrial Exhibition, held in the Klementinum in Prague in 1791. This exhibition, in which 4616 exhibitors took part and another 110 had their own separate stands, became not only a review of the past, but also a showcase of successful economic and cultural development and, what was most appreciated, a demonstration of the "enterprise of Czech spirit". As a result of the exhibition, national self-confidence was strengthened, especially due to the fact that the exhibition, originally planned to be regional with German attendance, turned out to be, thanks to the refusal of German businessmen to participate, an exclusively Czech affair.[14] Amongst the exhibitors were also 65 tailors, tailor's workshops and manufacturers of ready-made clothing and garments, 47 shoemakers and shoemaker's workshops, 10 furriers, 14 millineries, 9 glovemakers, 14 producers of ties, ribbons, plastic flowers and machine-knitted goods from the whole of Bohemia.[15] Exhibited items and a number of other attractions such as Křižík's electric tramway or newly-built viewing tower at Petřín Hill attracted 2 432 356 people to Prague, including school trips and compatriots from abroad.[16] The Exhibition of Czech - Slavic Etnography, which was set up in Výstaviště in Prague in 1895, was also met with wide acceptance. This exhibition presented Czech folk art in all its richness, diversity and charm. The success of the exhibition resulted in the founding of the Museum of Etnography and also of the association "Zádruha", which was also active in the field of textile production inspired by folk art. The influence of folk art after the exhibition was apparent in all branches of arts and crafts as well as in architecture. However, initiators of the exhibition were disappointed that folk patterns did not become common in either industrial production or decorative art, but together with new styles it gave way to cheap foreign imitations ranging from art nouveau to cubism.[17]

Cyclist.
Bohemia 1896.
Photo.
The Museum
of Physical Education
and Sport in Prague.

Contestants of ski race in Krkonoše Mountains.
Around 1905. Photo. The Museum
of Physical Education and Sport.

Horse races in Chuchle.
Pařížské Mody 1894, p. 167.

Fencing duel.
Bohemia around 1902.
Photo. The Museum
of Physical Education
and Sport in Prague.

The newly built Výstaviště exhibition park was not inactive during the following years - the Exhibition of Architecture and Engineering took place there in 1898 and there was a Anniversary Exhibition of the Chamber of Trade and Commerce in 1908, which provided a complete survey of historic, architectural, economic and cultural development in Prague over last few years. The production of mostly Prague's men's and ladies' clothing, garment and fashion accesories was also richly presented in this exhibition.[18]

The rise of the new century sees the Czech nation fully established in political, economical, cultural, social and art spheres. The aim of an "advanced, intelligent, conscious and rich society of all Czech classes"[19] was then to open up to a modern European lifestyle. The enterprising spirit of the last two decades of the 19th century, continued and the building of representative stands proceeded even further - at that time in a new style, whose name, as Jan Herain wrote in 1908, "was still to be found. At the beginning it was called secesse and now it calls itself "modern" in order to meet with a widescale acceptance and a positive response. Who would not like to be modern in order not to be oldfashioned?".[20] The Obecní Dům was, amongst other buildings, a fine example of art nouveau style. It was a representative house of the royal city of Prague, which provided a modern concert and ball hall as well as a number of other rooms for exhibitions and other social events for the use of the Prague public. The new art style was manifested not only in architecture, but it also in exhibition halls, which were up to that time reserved for anniversary exhibitions of art societies and museums. The new style soon established close contacts with most modern movements of world art and later demonstrated

Photo-Studie (modell)
pro umělce, nejkrásně
a skutečně umělecké ser
Nádherný katalog se 200
miniatur franko, uzavřen
Jen proti předem zaslá
pošt. znám. za 2 K.
Sklady „NOVITAS"
34 Rue Bellefond, Paris I

ZBRANĚ A KOLA
na splátky, součástí lev. l
ceníky zdarma. F. Dušek
továrna zbraní, kol a šicíc
strojů v Opočně čís. 187 n
státní dráze. Zástupci na pro
visí a plať se přijmau.

Pivní tlakostroje!
Elektrická čerpadla
vzduchu.
= Stáčecí stroje =
vyrábí a se zárukou prodává
A. Kučera, Praha VII. čp. 720.
Ceníky zdarma a franko.
Telefon 746/VI.

the ability of Czech artists to make significant contributions to them. Music and theatre life developed even further in connection with numerous guest performances of world-class stars. However, culture is not all that modern man lives for - sporting activities were also quickly coming into favour. Sporting activities in Bohemia had a long tradition. The physical training association Sokol, which was founded in 1862, was still very popular and regularly run its rallies. Football, watersports, cycling, lawn-tennis and also athletics and fencing were all commonly pursued, and Czech sportsmen took part in the Olympic Games, in 1912 even under a flag with a sign "Bohemia".[21] Young men started to appreciate the beauties of winter sports such as skiing and women were also soon captivated by sports and physical education. The Physical Education Society of Prague Women and Girls was founded in 1869 on the initiative of Dr. Miroslav Tyrš. Women took pleasure in swimming or, at least, bathing, skating, lawn-tennis and cycling. Cycling was a favourite activity of the famous opera singer Emma Destinová in times when she was still using her maiden name Kittlová.[22] Women with skis also followed men into the mountains, rarely at the end of the 19th century, but more often at the beginning of the 20th century. The first car exhibitions within the Empire took place in Prague. The city also organized horse races in order "to maintain the metropolitan character of the city and to increase the number of visitors".[23] Foreigners were, indeed, showing a great interest in Prague (the city was visited by 142 497 tourists[24] in 1908), despite complaints about the quality of services in the tourist industry in 1905.[25] The metropolitan character of Prague was also underlined by a number of newly opened restaurants, cafés and also entertainment halls such as Montmartre in Řetězová street, which was founded in 1911, or Tabarin and Alhambra, which were the first places in Prague where modern dance styles like "Maxixe Brasilienne", "Tao-tao", "Two-step" and tango became common. Before the First World War, the tango predominated society life in Prague - there were even advertisements for corset "tango" and dress "tango", which had a purple-red colour. Tango dance style was taught at dancing schools and the Vinohradské Theatre prepared an original operette of R. Piskáček, "Madame Tango".[26]

Tango in Tabarin in the Palace of Lucerna in Prague. Český Svět 1914, no. 20, p. 25.

The position of women

What place in this process of historical changes belonged to the women? Was woman still only a "devoted, voluntary servant of her man, intellectually submissive to him, being just a reflection of his feelings and interests?"[27]
Important steps in the field of emancipation of the Czech women were taken between 1840 and 1860 amongst a range of Prague women writers and Czech intellectual families. A movement which aimed at education and social help was created and the foundations for girls' educational system were laid in 1863 when the City High School for Girls was founded. A remarkably positive role in women's movement was played by Vojta Náprstek, who returned back to Prague after forcibly spending 10 years in United States in 1858. He was full of new modern ideas about creating a new society. He went to the World Exhibition in London in 1862 and came back with a number of technical inventions, which were later supposed to become the first exhibits of the Museum of Industry. These instruments for scientific purposes, machines and tools for craftsmen and devices for domestic work were later shown at the Industrial Exhibition at Střelecký island. Vojta Náprstek also organized a series of lectures on this occasion. They were attended also by women, who were especially interested in devices which made hard domestic work easier. Vojta Náprstek also informed women about the ideals of the world feminist movement and they later joined his programme with the "Address of Czech Women" in which they expressed their determination to learn and study despite the ridicule it would cause. In 1865 Náprstek reacted by founding of the American Club of Czech Ladies which, besides other activities, helped to formulate a programme for the Czech feminist movement according to foreign standards and with regard to the specific social situation in Bohemia. Membership of the club was free of charge and the only duty for members was self-education, charity work and youth care. Vojta Náprstek positively contributed to the education of women. His library, which contained at the end of the 19th century about 50 000

American Club
of Czech Ladies.
Photo. Around 1870.

Eliška Krásnohorská.
Drawing Jan Vilímek.
Zlatá Praha 1884, p. 345.

volumes, was opened twice a week strictly for women and he also continued to organize lectures on various topics. These lectures met with a huge response as the figures reveal: 575 lectures took place between 1865 and 1885 and they were attended by 26 750 women.[28/] The Women's Productive Association became an important institution in the field of the education and social independence of women. It was founded by Karolina Světlá in 1871 and until 1906, during 35 years of its existence, it educated over 20 000 girls and enabled them to undertake independent gainful employment.[29/] In 1881, the Productive Association had 5 classes in which 513 girls were taught by 25 teachers. The institution was divided into schools of commerce, drawing, languages with lectures in French, German, English and Russian, the school of hand work and additional department. Together with the Association of Czech Doctors the Women's Productive Association organized courses in the care of the ill in 1873 and it also conducted an employment office as well as a shop, which sold products of Association members and other goods such as "Erzgebirge" lace. Starting in 1873, the Women's Productive Association also published the magazine "Ženské Listy", which was edited by Eliška Krásnohorská and served as a platform for expressing the emancipation ambitions of women for many years.[30/]

The German section of Prague's women inhabitants also had similar Productive Association, in which 446 girls studied in 1881.[31/]

In the last two decades of the 19th century, common understanding for women's struggle for economic independence increased and therefore a number of other women's associations were created. Among these were for example "Vesna" in Brno, founded in 1878, South-Bohemian "Vesna" in České Budějovice, the association Household with cooking school in 1885 and many similar girls' schools. The City School of Advanced Girls was founded in 1884 with the aim of providing a perfect training in sewing garments and clothing. The school also had a department of commerce with language courses, a literature department and workshop. A number of other commercial and pedagogical schools, both private and state, followed soon afterwards. Around 1900, the government supported the newly-founded lyceums - a kind of girls' school similar to realschule and girls' high school. Finally, the first Girls' Academy of Commerce was opened in 1906 - 1907.

Teaching became the first profession available for women from the middle class when, according to the law of 1869, women were allowed to take up teaching jobs at public schools. Soon after teaching women made their way into the postal services (in 1872) and later into banking, insurance and commercial services. Women working manually created their own Organization of Working Women in 1897.[32/] Despite the uncommon increase in women's

= Hany Dumkové =
„Česká kuchařka"
vychází v sešítech po 16 h.

emancipation, university education remained unavailable to women as there was no secondary school for girls to prepare them for university studies. Eliška Krásnohorská took up this challenge and after long discussions with male Czech intellectuals and negotiations with official authorities she succeeded in founding a private secondary school, called Minerva, in 1890. This school, where girls finished their studies by sitting leaving exams and were awarded with a school leaving certificate, enabled girls to study at universities.[33/] The first title of Doctor of Philosophy in the Austro-Hungarian Empire was awarded to M. Baborová in 1901 and the first woman medical doctor studying in Prague, A. Honzáková, finished her university education in 1902. Her predecessors in this profession, A. Bayerová, B. Kecková and M. Kurková studied in Switzerland. In 1908, there were 24 female graduates of the Faculty of Philosophy in Prague and 8 female medical doctors.[34/]
However, an important event came in 1906, when Dr. Marie Peigertová undertook the job of medical registrar in the new children's hospital in Prague. She was the first-ever woman in such a position.[35/]
As far as art was concerned, the idea of women as actresses, singers and musicians had always belonged to Czech cultural life and, at the end of the 19th century, women writers did not have to fight for their position either. Women with talent for graphics acquired the possibility for professional education in 1885, when the School of Decorative Arts was founded.
The feminism movement found platforms for expressing their views in various women's magazines. Besides "Ženské Listy", which was, together with a similar English magazine, the oldest of its kind in Europe, there existed magazines such as "Ženský obzor", "Česká hospodyně" (1900), "Ženský svět", "Ženská revue", "Šťastný domov" (1904), "Česká dívka"(1904) and others. Women, led by Eliška Krásnohorská, expressed their political demands after the Anniversary Exhibition in 1891.[36/] Their request for suffrage was prompted by their struggle for freedom of education, the right to paid employment and also the struggle to gain greater independence in decisions about their children, which had been until then exclusively in the hands of the father.[37/] The Czech Women's Club, founded in 1904, had political as well as social programmes. The club associated women of all political views and all classes such as F. Plamínková, F. Zemínová, M. Tůmová, Dr. A. Honzáková, Ch. Masaryková and A. Masaryková and A. Leichterová.

🖙 Ženy české! 🖙
Krušné doby prodělává náš národ. Jedna nečistá aféra za druhou se provaluje, špinavého prádla je všude dost a dost. A tu se táži: Kdo je na prvním místě povolán, aby toto špinavé prádlo vypral? Zajisté, že jste to Vy, české ženy, které se nyní musíte pustit do obrodné práce a špinavé prádlo hamižných mužů vyprati. Je to práce veliká, práce nevděčná, ale co platno, prádlo se prát musí! Budete-li práti aparátkem »Pegoudem«, bude Vám to však hračkou; vyperete sněhobíle, bez namáhy, uspoříte práce, mýdla, ušetříte svých rukou a prádla. A ještě si při tom zazpíváte! — Prací aparátky »Pegoud« vyrábí a prodává po 8 K firma **Josef Lonský**, továrna kovového zboží, Roudnice n. L.

"Ladies Painting School"
at the School of Decorative Arts
in Prague. Český Svět 1905,
p. 233.

After demonstrations in 1905, the Committee for Women's Suffrage was founded. The long-lasting struggle paid off in 1912, when the first woman, writer B. Viková-Kunětická, was elected into regional parliament.[38/] However, women attained suffrage in 1920, after the independent Czechoslovakian state was founded in 1918.

The modern era brought not only the struggle for bigger social and economic independence, but it also brought fresh air into the old dominium of women's activity - household and family life. Spacious sunny apartments in newly-built districts of Prague with a water supply system, bathrooms and flushing toilets, which finally started to work properly after the completion of the construction of the water pumping station in Podolí in 1885, the cleaning and drainage of the city, new pavements with kerbs built in the 1870's, the introduction of an public electric lighting system in 1894 and an electric tramway in 1896, the planting of new parks - all these things contributed to the satisfaction of the demands for modern hygiene. Newspapers and magazines were full of advertisements for various inventions such as washing and spinning machines, vacuum cleaners, oil-cookers, slow-combustion stoves and central heating.[39/] All these things made household work easier. Last, but not least, the winds of change blew into the field of the mental and physical education of children and, naturally, into the institution of marriage, where women called for greater independence and an equal relationship between both partners, in which "each would have a joyful understanding for the desires of the other".[40/]

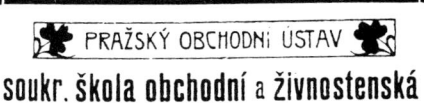

Čís. 50 Pohled ze předu na převěsek čís. I.

Dressing etiquette

The problems of women's social status were apparent in their appearance, behaviour and dress. Women's life fluctuated between restrictive prejudice and the heated struggle to reach their own identity and, similarly, the style of dress at the turn of the 19th and the 20th centuries was characterized by the struggle between the intricacy of conventional fashion kept within a framework of strict etiquette and the demands of modern hygiene, efficiency and purposefulness.

Already in the 19th century, types of dresses were strictly divided according to the occasion for which they were used. Between the 1870's and the 1890's fashion magazines published designs of home dress, lounge dress, dress for the morning walk, lunch dress, dress for the afternoon walk, tea dress, dinner dress, dancing ball dress, dress for Confirmation, wedding dress, mourning dress, dresses for teenage girls and mature ladies, dress for travelling, dress for the spa, dress for the seaside, maternity dress (which was called a dress for young ladies), and also designs of garment and sportswear.

The article "Ettiquette in Toilettes", which was published simultaneously in "Nové Pařížské Mody" in Prague and in Wiener Mode in Vienna on 1 December 1907, brought certain order to all the above-mentioned terms - it set out the difference between dresses for outdoor use and lounge toilettes and these two main groups were further divided. Outdoor dresses included dress for walks made preferably from English material with short skirt and plain blouse similar to a chemise, a smallish bonnet of subdued colours with a veil over the face, gloves from plain or chamois leather, a parasol and handbag. It also included dresses for both morning and afternoon walks which were made preferably from cloth, velvet or taffeta and consisted of an embroidered waistcoat with collar, full-length skirt and blouse, which, if worn, had to be made from lace, muslin or silk. Accessories for dresses for walks were also immodest - a fur-boa or plumage, a gold, silver or preferably leather handbag, and gloves from glossy or Swedish leather. Having a party with guests was also quite a complicated

Bazar 1892, p. 48.

Bazar 1870, p. 92.

Čís. 46—55. En tout cas. Slunečníky a hůlky na slunečníky.

V. J. Havlíček a bratr v Poděbradech. Račte si psáti o vzorky.

Vývozní dům lněného a modního zboží doporučuje v osvědčených a chvalně známých jakostech

Modní látky vlněné i prací, damské i pánské, plátna, damašky, ubrusy, ručníky zaručeně stálobarevné, překrásných moderních vzorů.

Zefíry na košile šaty atd. **Výbavy pro nevěsty**

za levné pevné ceny. — Velkolepý výběr. — Mnoho pochvalných uznání. Objednávky přes 15 K vyplaceně. 1 balík 40 m pracích zbytků vkusně rozdružené za 18 K. Franko dobírkou. Jen u nás ty pravé.

Č. 62. Kuchyňská zástěrka z režného plátna. Pohled s předu. (K vyobr. č. 61.) Střih na zadní str. příl. střih. č. XVI., fig. 48—50.

Č. 65. Černá grogrénová zástěrk ozdobená krajkovým vyšíváním. Střih a vzor na zad. str. příl. střih. č. XVII., fig. 51.

Dress for confirmation (dark)
and for communication (light).
Bazar 1878, p. 35.

matter - visits were always paid between 5 and 7 o'clock in the evening on a specific day and guests should be received in the heated lounge with flowers, tea-urn, roll with butter and plenty of sweets. The housewife was dressed in something between a fantastic tea-gown and the strict dress for special occasions such as visits. The dress was made from nice airy materials of light colours and lace. Tatty clothes, home dress or blouse were not suitable for receiving visitors as they would suggest the lack of a housewife's appreciation for her guests. Elegant lounge evening dress was made from high-quality material and had to consist of a train, a bonnet with ostrich feathers, gathered gloves from white or other light colour leather, an airy sash, boa, handbag, muslin muff and lace. Toilettes for the opera, theatre and concerts were made from muslin, crêpe de Chine and lace and included large hats. Serious suits of subdued colours without low-cut tops were recomended for theatre occasions. Toilette for concerts was similar to elegant dress for walks - dresses with necklines

řádek: vždy střídavě jako 4. a 5. řádek, avšak prvních a posledních 7 oček platí vždy střídavě ve 2 řádcích jako hladká, ve 2 řádcích jako obrácená (tato očka se upletou až k hrdelní okrouhlině týmž způsobem). — 28. a 29. řádek: očka platí na lícní straně jako obrácená. — 30. a 31. řádek: očka platí na rubu jako hladká. — 32. řádek: vždy střídavě 2 očka hladká, 2 obrácená. — 33. řádek: očka se upletou tak jako se jeví na této straně upletená. — Nyní se opakuje předně ještě 17kráte 20. až 33. řádek, při čemž se střídá hladkými a obrácenými očko 32. řádku, potom se pracuje pro levý zadkový díl na zevnějších 71 očkách ještě 8 opakování a ujme se při tom na konci 1. řádku každého opakování pro průramek 1 očko; potom následují pro raménka ještě 4 opakování bez ujímání, avšak v nejbližším nazpětjdoucím řádku nechá se posledních 31 oček, potom v každém následujícím nazpětjdoucím řádku

Čís. 68. Halenkovitá-košilka ze skotského zefíru s odpínacím límcem.
Střih a vysv. na zadní str. příl. Čís. XI.
Fig. 64—71.

Čís. 69. Elegantní spodnička z dykyty glacé.
Střihový přehled Fig. III.—VI. a vysv. na přední str. příl.

Bazar 1897, p. 80.

and a modern stylish haircut instead of a hat were accepted for evening concerts. Low-cut outfits and haircuts decorated with aigrettes or other fashionable accessories were recommended for dancing balls, dinners and evening parties. It was important to cover the hands and legs according to the style of the whole toilette. Certain things were completely unacceptable, these included low-cut wedding dresses at the morning ceremony, light ladies shoes worn with the evening lounge dress, fishnet gloves for visits and train or hat with feathers for walks and rainy weather.[41/]

Articles about appropriate dress continued to appear in the later issues of the magazine. The article called "Etiquette in Toilettes for Various Occasions" introduced suitable dress for a wedding ceremony - a white dress laced up to the neck, the indispensable train, white ladies shoes, gloves and book of prayers bound in ivory, pearl or white leather. Guests were also supposed to wear stiff dresses which would show taste, elegance and beauty, but were not meant to have the character of dress for dancing balls. The bride was also allowed to wear a dress for travelling, but thus she was deprived of the best memories of her life as "there is nothing as moving and beautiful as the bride standing in front of the altar in a white dress".[42/]

Even stricter rules applied to mourning occasions. Mourning dress had to be made from black smooth or rough woollen materials without a shine, the only accepted decorations were applications from crinkled English crepe. Cuts were more simple than the ones of the common dresses, a smooth bodice and skirt in the English style and decorated with crepe were recommended. During the second part of the mourning period it was possible to remove the crepe decorations and replace them with not very shiny silk ones. A veil was always essential for mourning, it was long, made from English crepe, flowing from the hat and covering the face for the death of parents and close relatives, and short from matt gauze with crepe fringe for the death of other relatives. How long was the mourning period? Two years for the widow, deep mourning for the first

Č. 48. Svatební oblek z atlasu a ze surahoviny. Pohled na přední stranu. (K tomu č. 25.) Střih a vysvětl. na zadní str. příl. str. č. VIII, fig. 40—46.

Č. 49. Salonní oblek z failloviny. Vysvětl. na zadní str. příl. str.

Bazar 1879, p. 173.

Bazar 1892, p. 136.

Čís. 68 a 69. Převěsek a klobouk z anglického krepu.
Čís. 70 a 71. Šaty a klobouk smuteční.
Čís. 72 a 73. Kép a klobouk smuteční.

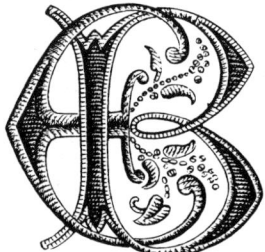

Čís. 24. Monogram.

s. 48. Pohled ze zadu na šaty čís. 13.

year, the following half year middle deep mourning with black dress and short veil and during the last half year the black dress could be decorated with white. After the death of parents deep mourning was kept for the whole year, another half year of middle deep mourning and in the last quarter of the year a black dress with white or grey decorations could be worn. Gold jewellery was not accepted during the whole of the mourning period, however jewellery from black pearls or onyx was accepted.[43] Dressing etiquette was observed in a number of other occasions such as the unveiling of monuments and others. Nevertheless, the magazine "Nové Pařížské Mody" calculated with still more solemn occasions and another of its articles introduced readers into the etiquette of dressing at the Imperial Court in Vienna.[44]

Úprava hostiny.

Posluha u stolu, úprava stolu, kladení ubrousků, k drůbeže a zvěřiny. S množstvím vyobrazení. Cena
Knihkupectví Al. Hynka v Praze, Celetná

MILOSTIVÁ!

Vkusná botička jest zajisté korunou elegance každé dámy!

Prohlédněte si laskavě můj **sklad** a shledáte určitě, že výrobky mé továrny jsou chloubou domácího našeho průmyslu.

Zásadou mou jest: dobré zboží, ochotná obsluha v každém směru, obchodování při menším výdělku a získání stálého kruhu odběratelstva.

Neopomenete zajisté navštívíte příležitostně můj podnik.

Obchodní dům s obuví

J. ŠLEMR,

v Jindřišské ulici č. 17, nároží Panské ul.

Objednávky na venek vyřizuji se obratem.
Stačí udání délky chodidla v centimetrech.

Opravy levně a ryohle!

Čís. 58—60. Střevíce modní.

Čís. 58—60. Střevíce modní.

Střevíc čís. 58 jest ze zlatohlavové usně na nártu vyšíváním krášlen. Spony střevíce jsou opatřeny dirkami, kterýmiž se provlíkne stuha u konců perlami zdobená, která se do vázanky sváže. Stuha jest 62 cm. dlouhá a 4½ cm. široká.

Čís. 59 jest střevíc z černé lakované usně, zdobený na nártu vyšíváním ze zlatých a ocelových i bílých perlí voskových; nad vyšíváním přišita jest vázanka atlasová a gumovka k upevnění střevíce jest zdobena podobnou vázankou.

The struggle of reform

The spirit of reforms proceeded very slowly in Bohemia, although ideas about the obnoxiousness of contemporary tight-fitting dresses emerged into the awareness of the professionals as well as the common public already in the 1890's. The first critical opinions appeared in connection with underwear in 1890, when the fashion magazine Bazar appraised that "producers claim that the shape of the body would no longer be determined by the bodice, but, on the contrary, the bodice would be made in order to fit the body. A creditable principle, indeed."[45] In 1894, Bazar magazine expressed satisfaction with contemporary fashion which avoided the unnatural squeezing of certain body parts and started to respect the needs of health and hygiene.[46] The Czech doctor Jaroslav Květ also watched the issue closely in the series of his articles such as "Doctor's opinion on ladies toilette" and "More facts about the corset" and others, which were published in "Nové Pařížské Mody" in 1894. He referred to the commentary of Jan Neruda called "Woman", in which the author admired Mrs Weiss and her shop in Vienna, who produced, displayed and sold corsets that fitted the individual needs of customers. Dr Květ also mentioned the harmfulness of a number of items of ladies garderobe such as small hats, suspenders and tight shoes.[47] The first kind of dress which accepted the spirit of change, was home dress, later called tea-gown. These dresses had comfortable princess cuts and inside they were fitted with a bodice without busks. Another type of dress, under which only a loose corset was worn, was a sporting dress. On 16th December 1892, Bazar magazine published a note about the first design of what would eventually become the modern bra.

Designs of top dresses, which were considered to be reformist, appeared in fashion magazines in the first years of the 20th century. At that

Bazar 1893, p. 35.

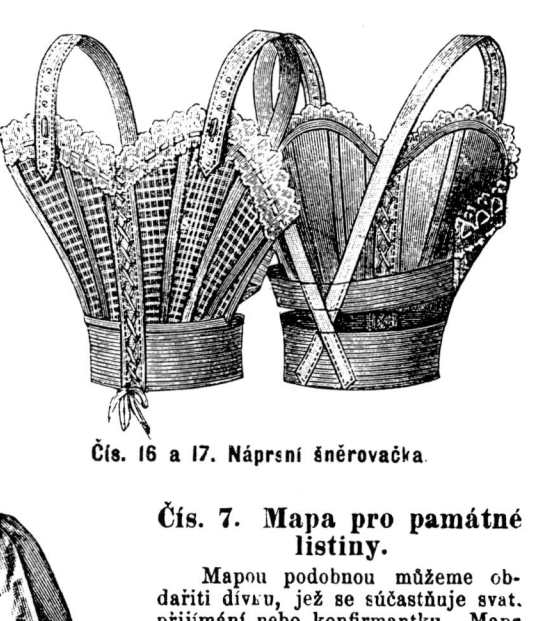

Pařížské Mody 1894.

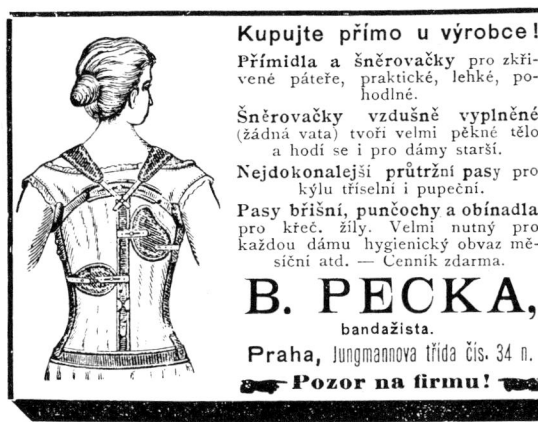

Kupujte přímo u výrobce!

Přímidla a šněrovačky pro zkřivené páteře, praktické, lehké, pohodlné.

Šněrovačky vzdušně vyplněné (žádná vata) tvoří velmi pěkné tělo a hodí se i pro dámy starší.

Nejdokonalejší průtržní pasy pro kýlu třeselní i pupeční.

Pasy břišní, punčochy a obínadla pro křeč. žíly. Velmi nutný pro každou dámu hygienický obvaz měsíční atd. — Cenník zdarma.

B. PECKA,
bandažista.

Praha, Jungmannova třída čís. 34 n.

Pozor na firmu!

opatřme ho okrasou a napřed skrytou háčkovou uzavírkou, napřed u pravého předního kraje přišijme hnědé hedvábné šňůrové smyčky a na levé straně vhodné knoflíky. Jsou-li naštepovány druhé přednice v zadu na šůsku a v zadkových dílech až k čáře, podložme šůsek dykytovou podšívkou a přišijme k živůtku límec, jenž se musí při tom trochu vytáhnouti a přeložiti podél čáry k zevnějšku. Posléze ozdobme rukávy a všijme je do průramků.

Čís. 34. Sportovní úbor pro dívky.

Bílého anglického plátna je užito ke zhotovení tohoto švihackého úboru, jenž je ozdoben naštepovanými modrými plátěnými pruhy a doplněn bílým usněným pasem a plaveckou čapkou. Hladká sukně je lemována dole třemi příčnými pruhy, kdežto okrasa volné halenky tvoří podélné pruhy, jež se opakují skupinovitě napřed a v zadu. K námořnickému límci je připojena napřed modrá nákrčenka, ozdobená bílými vydutinovými švy. Výstřih halenky je vyplněn náprsníkem, ozdobeným modrými pruhy.

Čís. 35. Pláštěnka s okrasou z třásní.

Tato elegantní krátká pláštěnka jeví velmi slušný tvar a je zhotovena z bílé dykyty, povlečené černým gázem s pailetkovým vyšíváním, jehož vzor se liší velmi působivě od světlého podkladu. Pláštěnka je přistřižena v zadu do špičky, ku předu vzestupně a připojena

Čís. 44. Klobouk a vyšívaný límec s perlovými třásněmi.

Vyobrazením tímto je znázorněn jemný bílý slaměný klobouček pro mladou dámu, jenž činí pravý letní dojem; okrasa kloboučku skládá se z hladké široké aksamítky a veliké kytice velerudých makových květů, jejichž barvoskvostnost je oživena ještě žlutými a zelenými klasy. — Rovněž tak elegantní a nová je tato náhrdelní okrasa, která se hodí zvláště k doplnění hladkých živůtků, jimž je dodáno zcela nový ráz. Okrasa skládá se z černého aksamítového a lehce zaokrouhleně přistřiženého límce, jenž je pošit

Čís. 36—38. Šaty, klobouk a havelok k vycházkám v lázních, na cesty atd.
Střih, vzorový nákres a vyšv. na přední str. příl. Čís. I. Fig. 1—13.

ocelovými broušenými cetičkami a opatřen napřed podlouhlými, pobočně dvěma okrouhlými ocelovými ornamenty. Od límce tohoto dopadají asi 20 cm dlouhé třásně z ocelových perel, jež jsou pošity napřed velmi těsně.

Čís. 46. Šaty a klobouk pro dívky od 15—16 let.

Tyto roztomilé letní šaty ze světlomodře a černě tečkovaného vlněného batistu jsou ozdobeny velmi působivě bílou dykytou a bílými krajkovými vložkami a zoubečky. Sukně je ozdobena třemi řasnatými, 5 cm širokými podlinami, lemovanými zoubečky a je upravena k zapínání v zadu nad řasnatým halenkovým živůtkem. Nášev je kryt bílým dykytovým pasem, jenž je zakončen v zadu pod bohatými krátkými vázankami a dlouhými konci s třásněmi (viz též malý pohled ze zadu náčrtkem c). Živůtek je též upraven v zadu k zapínání a jeví bílé dykytové, v zadu okrouhlé, napřed špičaté tílko, ušité v podélné lemy, k němuž je připojen podobný stojatý límec, jenž je přistřižen pobočně v ostré špičky, lemován zoubečky a ušit též v úzké lemy. Okraj

Čís. 39 a 40. Nová spodnička a náprsní držadlo.
Střih a vyšv. na zadní str. příl. Čís. XIII. Fig. 115 a 116 jakož i zmenšená střihová předloha Fig. I.—IV.

Bazar 1893, p. 82.

time, efforts to change clothing style abroad formed a united front, which manifested its existence in organizing various exhibitions. One such exhibition was organized by Verein für Verbesserung der Frauenbekleidung in Berlin in 1899, reformist fashion was also displayed at the Kunst und Kunstgewerbe exhibition in Dresden and many other fashion exhibitions soon followed in German towns. The International Exhibition of Reformist Fashion took place in Vienna in 1907 and the Association of Public Health Service in Prague came up with the demand for a change of clothing style in the same year. The creation of women's dress, which would be ideal as far as both hygiene and aesthetics was concerned, was pursued by such remarkable artists as Henry van de Velde, Petr Behrens and Gustav Klimt. Despite all of this pressure, expressed also by numerous publications of reformistic dress in fashion magazines, ladies and the general public showed little enthusiasm for the oncoming change. This attitude was spelled out by Joža Potocká in 1906: "In spite of massive suggestions for abolishing the bodice, it is essential to wear it under such new dress, even more essential than under the blouse and tight-fitting skirt, if woman do not want to look as if wearing a negligé. Taking into account the needs of hygiene, these new dresses are simply laughable because of their length - they even go with magnificent train. The sleeves are also very impractical." [48]

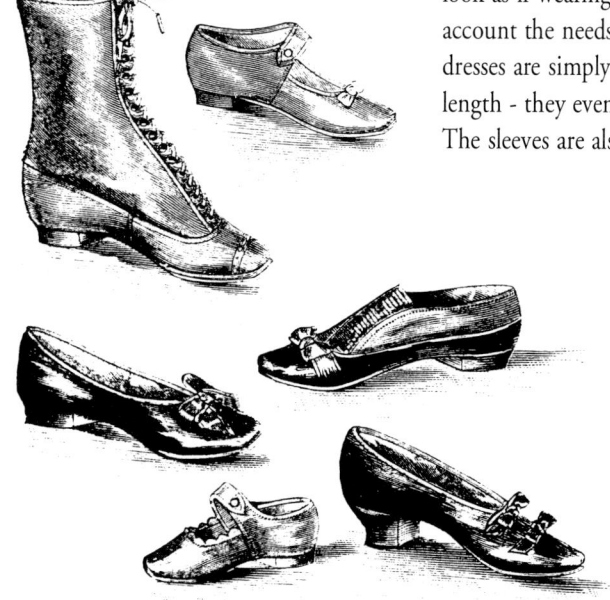

Čís. 12—18. Modní obuv.

Production and trade

What was the development of the tailor trade? While in 1881 there were altogether 743[49] tailors in Prague, in 1896 there were 976 men's tailors and 38 men's fashion shops, 581 ladies' tailors and 81 fashion shops for ladies.[50] By 1910, this number had further increased to 1661 men's tailors, 1317 ladies tailors and 147 shops with ladies' ready-made clothing. Other producers were registered in categories of trade with ladies blouses, tricot suits and fashionable goods.[51] These figures can not be accurate as some producers were registered in different trade categories and some of the tailors provided services for both men and women. Furthermore, the difference between producers and tradesmen can not be clearly identified. We also have to take into account that the increase in these figures was partly caused by the fact that Prague as a city grew in size with the affiliation of surrounding villages. However, contemporary directories clearly show a steady increase in tailor production.

As many advertisements in the contemporary press reveal, tailor's workshops worked to order as well as for stock. In the second half of the 19th century, besides these little workshops there was also a successful expansion of the large-scale production of ready made clothing, whose centre was in Prostějov, a town in Moravia. Large scale production was applied first to men's and children's wear and later, in the 1880's and the 1890's, also in the production of ladies' wear - above all in top wear such as jackets, top coats, raincoats and, towards the end of the 19th century, also in costumes.[52]

Besides a number of new shops, there was also the development of the department store. Two remarkable department stores were mentioned in contemporary press reviews.

The first one was built in Příkopy street no.4

Dům Filipa Haas-e a synů na Příkopech v Praze. (Kreslil J. Scheiwl.)

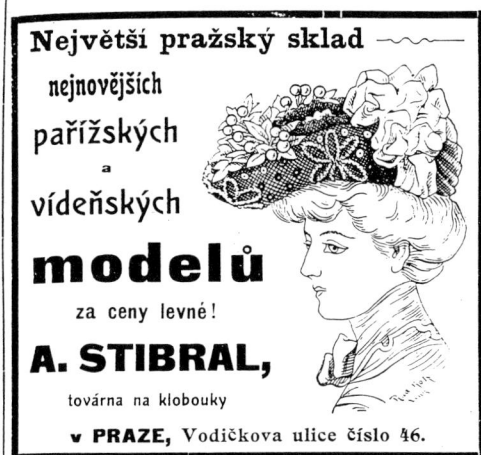

for the carpet and indoor textile trade company Philipp Haas and sons between 1869 and 1870. The construction was made from cast iron and such features as an open space with multiarmed staircase and inside equipment such as a water supply system, elevators, home telegraph and gas lighting made it one of the most modern department stores in Europe, completed even earlier than Bon Marché in Paris.[53/] Another famous building of this kind was the department store of J. Novák called "U Štajgrů", which was designed by Oswald Polívka and built in Vodičkova street between 1902 and 1903. This department store contained selling space in the assembly hall, columned hall and in the galleries, where a wide selection of textiles, ready-made clothing, accessories, furniture, cosmetics, Chinese and other foreign goods was sold. It was also equipped with reading rooms with Czech and foreign magazines, a study room for customers, changing rooms, a spacious buffet, stores, offices and dressing rooms for staff. For the contemporaries, who were very enthusiastic about the building, the department store of J. Novák symbolized another step towards fulfilling the desire for national independence.[54/] A lot of robes with labels of the Viennese work-shops preserved in the collection of the Museum of Decorative Arts give evidence of the vivid contacts between the Viennese fashion design, cultivated especially among the aristocratic circles that lived both in Vienna and Bohemia. On the other hand - a large number of the Czech names on the list of Viennese tailors prove that Bohemia was supplying Vienna with qualified craftsmen able to survive in competition.[55/]

The department store
of J. Novák in Prague,
Český Svět 1904,
no. 3, p. 124.

Dámská a dětská konfekce.

Vlastní výroba žaketů, pláštěnek atd.

Též z přinesených látek se šaty zhotovují.

EMILIE HAVRDOVÁ
na Král. Vinohradech,
Palackého třída č. 25. n.

Vzorný dámský akademický ústav.

Nejchvalnější pověsti se těšící odborná škola v Praze ku theoretickému a praktickému vyučování **kreslení střihů** a braní míry dle mé vlastní, nedostižné soustavy ve 2—3 dnech, šití a aranžování dámských úborů v 1 až 6 měsících. Dámám možno nastoupiti denně a obdrží ku přání též celé vzorné zaopatření.

Současně upozorňuji na svoji na četných výstavách prvními cenami vyznamenanou odbornou knihu: „Umělý samouk střihů", co jediná svého druhu v naší literatuře, taž vyšla již v 7. vydání a jest k dostání v mém. ústavě. Objednané střihy dle míry od 1 K výše. — Módní salon ku zhotovování dámských úborů. — Bližší v prospektech, jež ochotně zašle

Terinka Ptáčková,
majitelka ústavu a odborná spisovatelka v PRAZE, Myslíkova ulice č. 15

Odebírejte Dra. K. Maye: Odkaz posledního Inky.

Konfekce pro dámy vlastní výroby
FRANTIŠEK FRIML,
PRAHA, uprostřed Celetné ulice č. 30. n.,
proti kavárně »U červeného orla«.

Přízemí a mezipatro.

Kožešiny, jen pravé solidně spracované,
vždy novotiny **J. O. WONDRÁČEK,**
odporučuje firma
moderní kožešnictví a obchod s kožešinami,
PRAHA, Staré město, Malé nám. č. 459.
Založeno r. 1834. Telefon č. 544.

Kde

koupím nejlépe hotovou dobrou obuv? Doporučuji chvalně známou firmu

Rudolf Babánek,

sklad veškerého druhu obuvi
pro dámy, pány a dítky
v Praze,
Jindřišská ulice
čís. 10,
vedle hlavní pošty.

Firma ta těší se velké oblibě mezi českým obecenstvem.

Zakázky z venkova vyřizují se na dobírku rychle a přesně a dostačí zaslání **pravé starší boty,** a udání přibližné ceny i druhu. — Nehodící se ochotně vymění.

302

Modní barchety.
Modní flanely.
Novotiny na bluzy.

Největší výběr, nejlevněji.

J. Novák „u Štajgrů".

Račte sobě výkladce prohlédnouti.

Obsah listu: Vyobrazení č. 1. až 5. Obleky letní pro dámy a děti. — 6. a 7. Obleky k vycházkám, zhotovené z látky mozambik a toile-de-laine (k tomu střih). — 8. a 9. Medailony k ozdobování desk a j. v. pestrobarevné. — 10. Kabelka na pletení s povlakem sítkovaným (k tomu střih). — 11. Růžice z frivolit a háčkování. — 12. Nárožní okolek ku kapesním šátkům, ochranným pokrývkám a pod. v. (Bílé vyšívání). — 13. límec z tylu a mulu (k tomu střih). — 17. Vzor sítkovaný k oponám, pokrývkám atd. — 18. až 30. Rozličné zástěrky (k tomu střih a vzor). 31. až 35. Rozličné životy a obleky do společnosti pro mladé dámy (k tomu střih). 36. Okolek k oponám, pokrývkám na oltáře atd. (Vyšívání krajkové a bílé). — 37. Háčkovaný okolek k ozdobování prádelních předmětů a pod. v. — 38. a 39. Živůtky pro dívky od 1 do 3 let (k tomu střih). — 40. opony (k tomu střih). — 41. Kabelka nad postel z vlněného rypsu (k tomu střih). — 42. a 43. Spony k oponám pletené a drhané z frivolit. — 44. a 45. Vzor k pletení na kabátky dětské, čepce, pokrývky atd. 46. ik na ruční práce, klíče a pod. v. (k tomu střih). — 48. a 49. Nárožní okolek k ozdobování lambrekýnu, polštářů a pod. v. (Vyšívání na kanavě). — 50. až 55. Fiží a jupka z tylu (k tomu střih).

Obsah střihové přílohy: { Střihy k vyobrazením č. 6., 7., 10., 13., 14., 15., 16., 18., 21., 22., 23., 24., 27., 28., 31. až 35., 38., 40., 41., 46., 58. Vzor k vyobrazení č. 22. až 28. Vysvětlení k vyobrazením č. 6., 7., 13., 14., 15., 16., 18. až 35., 38., 50., 51.

The fashion magazines

Knowledge of world fashion came to Bohemia mostly through fashion magazines, the publishing of which substantially progressed between the years 1870 and 1914.
In the previous section we witnessed the efforts of Antonie Melišová-Körschnerová to publish "Lada", the first women's magazine published in Czech between the years 1862 and 1864 with fashion designs which aimed at uniting the French mode with Czech folk costumes. This kind of attitude toward women's fashion was soon abandoned and later was mercilessly criticized by Eliška Krásnohorská, who blamed Melišová for creating caricatures and dilettantism.[56] The newly developing nation in the last quarter of the 19th century needed to demonstrate its "entrance to Europe" by the character of its clothing and needed to conform to European fashion. The first efforts to create an original women's fashion were continually unsuccessful. Between the years 1870 and 1872 magazine "Květy" published an independent fashion supplement called "Bazar" (The Bazar).
Its editor was Mrs Antonie Melišová-Körschnerová, who expressed her patriotic feelings by publishing fashion illustrations from French journals (Petit Courier des Dames and Journal des Demoiselles) and not German ones.[57] Some original designs by Mr Huttar and Mr Svoboda appeared only exceptionally. As soon as 1872 "Květy" lost in competition to "Světozor", which was overprinted as an independent fashion supplement by the German "Bazar", published in Berlin. It was issued in Czech simultaneously with the German version but without the German literary supplement. Only during the 1890's at the same time as the first fashion reports, did the independent information about the Czech fashion atmosphere appear in "Bazar" - for example some appreciation of Czech woollen clothes, a note on the Exhibition of Ethnography or on Moravian and Czech embroidery.[58] The editor of "Bazar" was for 20 years Mrs Ant. Melišová - Körschnerová, as we can discover from her necrolog, published in 1894.[59] Her successor was Mrs Anna Körschnerová, her sister. Mladá Boleslav became an important centre of fashion publishing, thanks to the publisher, book-shop owner and editor Karel Vačlena. Vačlena had satisfied a wide range of women's interests with his magazines - his fashion paper, published from 1879 to 1935 under the title "Modní Svět" (The Fashion World) was an overprint of the German magazine "Die Modenwelt" and besides the fashion itself it contained supplements "Světová Bibliotéka" (The World Biblioteque) and "Lada", the editor of which was a women writer and the first editor of "Ženské Listy" Mrs Věnceslava Lužická, and some other supplements - "Dětský modní svět" (The Child's Fashion World) and "Ruční práce" (Handcraft). The second magazine, issued in his publishing house from 1900 - "Damské Mody" (Woman's Fashion), also had several supplements. Between the years 1899 and 1904 Vačlena also published a men's fashion magazine - "Elegantní kroj".
In December 1893 in Prague J.R. Vilímek started to publish "Pařížské Mody" (The Paris Fashion) - a paper for Czech ladies and girls, edited by Zdenka Maroldová from Paris. The

< Bazar 1871, no. 29, p. 108.

fashion editor was Mrs Zdislava Zapová, and for the literature part was responsible J.R.Vilímek himself. Among the interests of this magazine, besides fashion, there were also the problems of household, children education, education in general and some other aspects of a woman's world. It also published original fashion reports and information about events in Prague, Paris, Karlovy Vary and elsewhere in Bohemia, accompanied by French fashion illustrations.

In 1888 "Wiener Mode" magazine was founded in Vienna, and it became very popular throughout the Empire. Two years later in Prague the magazine "Nové Mody" (The New Fashion), appeared which was an overprint of "Wiener Mode" until 1893. In 1894 its orientation changed toward Paris. In 1895 both Prague magazines - "Pařížské Mody" and "Nové Mody" united under the title "Nové Pařížské Mody" (The New Paris Fashion) which, again, became the Czech version of the Viennese magazine "Wiener Mode". This magazine had two supplements - "Damské Besedy" (Ladies Talks) and "Dětská Šatna" (Children's Wardrobe). Other important and long existing magazines were French - oriented journals issued by the First Prague Academy to cultivate fashion and the tailor's art. "Damské Modní Listy" issued from 1901 to 1924, were dedicated to modern French dress and were published by Jan Kratina in co-operation with contributors from Berlin, Paris and Prague. A similar magazine, "Damské Akademické Modní Listy" (The Ladies Academic Fashion Papers) was the magazine issued by the Fisrt Prague Academy and was edited by Václav Kratina from 1899 to 1943.

The papers concentrated on the fact that the existing fashion magazines were more concerned with entertainment than professional matters and so the Papers aimed to inform and educate about all the demands of ladies' fashion from the professional point of view - they tried to show the originals of French fashion novelties "which are authoritative all over the civilized world", to distribute the professional knowledge of cut, arranging, sewing, and taking measurements for women's clothing. A parallel magazine, designed for men was "Akademické Modní Listy" (The Academic Fashion Papers), issued between 1898 and 1934 by Jan Kratina and edited by Václav Kratina. Their character was similar. Between 1911 and 1913 Jan Kratina issued also

Damské Modní Listy 1907, no. 6.

"Damský Modní Obzor" (The Ladies Fashion Horizon), and an illustrated family magazine for Czech ladies and girls, dealing with fashion, amusement and education. Between 1916 and 1922 he issued also "Pražský Modní Obzor" (The Prague Fashion Horizon). There was still one more women's fashion magazine that had survived for more than two decades - "České Mody" (The Czech Fashion) issued between 1910 and 1932, a pictorial magazine for Czech ladies and girls, published in Prague by KarelLočák and directed by Mrs Libuše Žižková. During the whole period there were attempts to found other fashion magazines, but none of them managed to survive for very long.

As far as it was possible to discover, all these

Dětské vozíky

v nejmodernější úpravě za ceny velice levné, též **niklování veškerých kovových předmětů**, jako vidliček, nožů atd. u

Aloise Řezníčka

Výroba dětských vozíků a galvaniscurství

v Karlíně,
Palackého tř. 28.

Jan Stoupa
v Praze,
na Václavském nám. č. 32.
nabízí 9

Haveloky  **Haveloky**

z jemného, nepromokavého štyrského lodenu, v barvě tmavošedé, šedohnědé, tmavoolivové, zhotovené přesně dle zde uvedeného výkresu

zl. 14·50.

Při ct. objednávkách vyprošuji si udání potřebné délky haveloku.

Zimníky od 30 zl. počínaje.
Kožichy ve vkusném střihu.
Nové lovecké kabáty od 15–35 zl. 646·5
Salonní kabáty od 25 do 45 zl
Haveloky a ulstry od 25–45 zl.
Dětské obleky a župany atd. za nejlevnější ceny doporučuje chvalně známý závod

M. Mottla synové,
c. k. dvorní dodavatelé

Mně darovalo prstýnek
děvčátko rozmilé, který koupilo u

VIL. SVATONĚ,
PRAHA-II., Žitná ul.
č. 23. n. (proti faře).

HODINY LEVNĚ!

Administrace „Evropských Mod" Praha

Ročník desátý.   Číslo I.   Duben 1871.

ZLATÉ DNO.

MÓDNÍ LIST PRO KREJČÍ.

Odpovědný redaktor a vydavatel:

VOJTĚCH ČIHAŘ

bytem v čísle 412.–I., roh Perlové a Rytířské ulice (Vaječného trhu).

Vychází ve dvou saisonách ročních a sice vždy v dubnu, květnu, červnu, pak v říjnu, listopadu a prosinci o velkém archu s četnými vyobrazeními a zvláštní litografovanou přílohou.

Předplatné přijímá se v bytu redaktorově a ve všech řádných knihkupectvích a obnáší pro Prahu: na obě saisony 2 zl. 50 kr., na jednu saisonu 1 zl. 25 kr.; poštou: na obě saisony 2 zl. 75 kr., na jednu saisonu 1 zl. 38 kr.; jednotlivá čísla jsou po 50 kr. —).

Centimetry (míry stotinné), jeden arch za 25 kr.; nastříhané a podlepené za 60 kr.

Veškeré dopisy k redakci přijímají se jen frankované, taktéž nezapečetěné listy reklamační nefrankují se.

Situace módy.

Co nám v Německu do nedávna ještě vytýkali, činí nyní s velkým ohněm sami i starají se o vlastní národní kroj svůj, aby nemusili říditi se ve všem vsudy dle národa francouzského. U nás vyrostl kroj moderně národní ze snahy, abychom dali výraz národní své bytosti, u Němců má vyrůsti z pouhé svrchované nenávisti naproti národu jinému; naše pohnutka byla nepoměrně čistší. Zábavno je dívati se, s jakým nadšením potácejí se do vynalezení německých mód národních, a jakým ohněm, ze ani nepozorují, že nakreslujíce v módních časopisech „německý kabát" vyobrazují vlastně kabát lužického sedláka, a kreslíce „německý klobouk" podávají obraz klobouku ruského, tak několik set let už starého. A při tom chválí jeden druhého „tlustým palcem" nejen pro důvtip a vynalezavost, nýbrž i pro „pravé vlastenecké nadšení".

Nescházelo tam ovšem také hlasů střízlivějších, třeba jich bylo málo. Mezi těmi je také hlas Jakoba Falka, z jehož historických pojednání o krojích a s nimi spojených mravech rozmanitých věků byli jsme v dřívějších letopisech „Zlatého dna" podali mnohou ukázku zajímavou. Nyní horlí proti německému kroji národnímu a celou tou prací, můžeme nyní tím spíše, že každé slovo svědčí ku prospěchu národního kroje českého. Falek nazývá kroj národní „ztranulou módou minulých věků", důkazem tedy nepokročilosti, mluví proti vynalezení fantastických forem zcela nových a vyhrávání forem až příliš zastaralých. Posledního zajisté přikládá sám nejmenší váhu, neboť co historik ví, že i nejnovější jakákoli móda bývá odleskem dob minulých a opakováním forem jejich — jest vůbec nesmírně těžko najiti něco zcela nového. Národní kroj český vyrostl sloučením evropského kroje moderního s příznaky a přídavky českými v našem národě oblíbenými. Nepříč se náhledem vzdělaného světa, ale podržuje zároveň i ráz svůj zvláštní, jako vzdělaná, i nejsvětoobčanštější, přece zůstává ve mnohém osobností zvláštní, člověkem s v ý m. A právě pro toto „sloučení" živé má u nás také móda čili pokrok (změna) zcela dobré místo své, není třeba žádného zastarání a ztrnutí a přece můžem při českém kroji setrvati. Všechny ročníky našeho časopisu podaly důkaz i pokroku moderního i setrvání v rázu národním zároveň.

Módní zpráva a objasnění módní přílohy.

Tímto číslem nastupuje „Zlaté dno" svůj desátý ročník. Mnohý tuhý boj museli jsme podstoupiti proti vetřelosti cizácké, chtíce by list náš způsob v kruzích českých zdomácněl. Nešetřili jsme skromných sil svých v zápasu pro věc dobrou a chceme i na dále raziti dráhu nezávislosti čtenářstva našeho v ohledu národním i životním.

Právě co toto psáti počínáme, těšíme se velmi příznivé jarní povětrnosti; než myslíme, že s v měsíci dubnu ještě chladných dnů dožijeme a dle toho také již módní přílohu pro měsíc duben sestavili. Nežli však k podrobnějšímu objasnění módní přílohy přikročíme, budiž nám několik slov o módě vůbec pronésti. Co se látek pro nastávající jarní saisonu určených tyče, nelze mnoho sděliti, jež to v ohledu tom aspoň žádné nápadné novoty nevyskytly; to co o nich s jistotou říci můžeme jest, že vynikají hlavně jednoduchostí i co do barvy i co do vzorů. Při kabátových látkách žádná barva nepřevládá; nejvíce se udržuje modrá, hnědá a zelená v rozličných odstínech.

Látky na kalhoty jsou nejvíce světlých barev a velmi jemných buď hlubokoavaných, kostkovaných neb žíhovaných vzorů; velmi elegantní jsou zcela hladké látky. Široké lampasy jež již přežily a tudíž buď zcela úzké neb žádné.

Ohledně vkusu vznáme následující: jarní a letní svrchník budiž co možná krátky a pouze na jednu řadu knoflíků k zapínání upraveny. Co se tyče salonního kabátu jedno- neb dvouradového chceme již čtyřry dlužno poznamenati, že se talíc nejvýše o jednu neb dvě stotiny prodloužiti smí: to však platí jen o něm zcela; fantastická žaketa nepodléhá žádnému zákonu; zde se ponechává úplná svoboda vyhověti obecenstvu dle jeho přání a potřeb. Že by posud trvající forma spodků nějaké změnu utrpěla, pochybujeme; neboť nynější forma jejich vyhovuje dostatečně i pohodlí i vkusu.

Co se konečně vesty tyče, musíme zase jen opakovati, co jsme již vícekrát pronesli, že se totiž nevyskytla ještě jiná forma, která by až posud trvající přemohla.

Postava 1.

V této spatřujeme pána mající na sobě světlohnědý kabát, jehož tale jen zcela nepatrné dle nejnovějšího vkusu a výše uvedeného pravidla prodloužena jest; spodky jsou světlé perlošedé barvy, drobně kostkované přírozené.

Postava 2.

představuje pána zcela černě oděného: má na sobě volný slovanský svrchník se širokými rukávy a s předmutým límcem, k zapínání jest upraven na spodky a kulaté knoflíky; kalhoty jsou široké, na způsob polských upraveny.

Postava 3.

jest pán, jehož celý oblek zvláštní elegantností vyniká; svrchník jemné vlnové barvy jest jak viděti lze do-cti volný, aby se pohodlněji svlékati a oblékati mohl; kalhoty jsou taktéž světlé barvy tmavými body proužkovány.

Postava 4.

V této spatřujeme pána v modrém dvouradovém salonním kabátě se širokým přeložením klop a límce a v přiléhacích spodkách barvy tabákošedé.

Postava 5.

jest pán oděn v tmavozelený jarní svrchník opatřený ukrytou podložkou, v níž se dírky k zapínání nalezají; kalhoty jsou jasné hnědé barvy, jemně žihované.

Postava 6.

představuje pána, jehož oblek pro častější vycházky z jedné a téže látky barvy ořechové upraven jest; má na sobě krátké poněkud přiléhací dvouřadové sako; po stranách jsou kapsy patkami opatřeny, v krajích jest hedvábnou tkanicí téže barvy obloženo.

Vysvětlení vzorů.

Fig. 1.—2.

jest vzor slovanského volného svrchníku, hodícího se velmi dobře pro postavu 2. dnešní módní přílohy.

Fig. 3.—4.

podává vzor francouzského svrchníku opatřeného podložkou, v níž dírky k zapínání nalezají a jehož pro postavu 5. na módní příloze označeno užíti lze.

Postava 5.—7.

naznačuje vzor fantastického volného saka bojně kapsami opatřeného, límce a klopy jsou potaženy hedvábným látkem, ve stranách a vzadu nalezají se rozparky, v krajích jest dvakrát prostepováno; podobného saka můze se velmi dobře užíti i pro převlek, pokli se ze stejných látek vyhotoví.

Fig. 8.—9.

přináší vzor dvouradového svrchníku, jehož límec a klopy na široké pošoženy vypcítány jsou; střih tento hodí se velmi dobře pro postavu 3. módní přílohy.

Fig. 10.—12.

podává vzor stále ještě oblíbeného tak zvaného bastardu.

Fig. 13.—18.
jsou vzory dvou kabátů na dvě řady knoflíků k zapínání upravených, jejichž límce a klopy na široko přeložení vypočítány jsou.

Fig. 19.—21.
naznačuje vzor oblíbené jednořadové žaketu s dosti širokým přeloženým klopem a límce po stranách patkami opatřené.

Fig. 22.—25.
jest vzor dvouřadového salonního kabátu, jehož klopy se široce překládají; kabát téhož střihu spatřujeme na postavě 4. módní přílohy.

Fig. 26.—28.
přináší vzor jednořadové žakety, nevyžadující bližšího vysvětlení.

Fig. 29.—30.
jsou vzory dvojích spodků, z nichž prvnější více vybrané a na botu přiléhající,

druhé zase více rovné jsou.
přílohy.

podávají vzory tří rozličných … lovým límcem, figura 32. zn … estrojujících mezi delší neb … stranní špičce atd., což vidí … mira předního poprsí k po … vzrůstu. Zcela jiným jest vša …

jest pohled na hotový již … sobě má.

poskytuje zase pohled na h … stavě 6 dnešní módní příloh …

Beseda.

Úplná soustava korporismetrie nebo-li nauky o brání míry.
(Pokračování.)

Jak již z pouhého pojmenování vysvítá, jde šířka slabin od švu zadku dole v životě přímo ku předu k slabině, nicméně ne tak daleko, až kde jest kost slabiny nejvyvinutější – nebot bod ten nalézá se obyčejně dále naprod — nýbrž toliko k místu, kde u kabátů s prodlouženým životem bývá pravidelně tak zvaný podpažní průstřih. Kaiserschnitt k švu zadku od středu uvažujeme dále, po té k místu, kde spolu končí míry poprsí, nazveme průranku další. Toto místo, kde spolu končí míry poprsí, nazveme bodem centrálním, kteréhožto pojmenování k snadnějšímu porozumění i budoucně užívati budeme.

Máme-li "tělomérný pás" a přiložili jsme jej tak, jak již při popisu pasu toho uvedeno, netřeba šířku slabin zvláště měřiti, neboť číslice, která se nalézá u centrálního bodu, udává správně šířku slabin. Šířka tato může býti při stejných šířkách na prsou velmi rozdílná, nebot vše závisí od toho, zdali šířka nad kyčli naproti šířce zadku skoro se vyrovná, či zdali šířka od slabin zadku jest buď menší neb větší a vůbec od způsobu držení těla.

U všech prostředně silných a souměrně rostlých osob jest šířka slabin pravidelně o 2—3 centimetry menší nežli šířka zadku. Poměr ten bývá i u osob tlustých a to v případech, kdy život není příliš plochý, nýbrž řádně vyvinutý, s čím se setkáváme u obyčejně u osob, jichž břicho z větší části ku předu jest vyvinuto. Naproti tomu bývá často i u prostředně silných osob šířka slabin větší a tudíž šířce zadku skoro se vyrovná, což bývá v případech, kdy dolejší šířka těla v poměru k hořejší jest značně vyvinuta, aneb když život jest příliš prohnutý, -odlehou více ve směr v šířce a šíři.

U dobře rostlých osob, mohlo by se říci, že šířka slabin obnáší dobrou ½ polovice šířky na prsou, ačkoliv za příčinou častých výminek nemožno se spoléhati na všechna tato pravidla, nýbrž nutno vždy zřetel míti k vzrůstu. Ostatně můžeme si pomocí podobných pravidel při braní míry velmi často zjednati rychlejšího a správnějšího přehledu. Za tou příčinou uvádíme zde pro veškeré šířky a délky těla jestě zcela určitá udání, při čemž zároveň vždy ohled vzat na šířku zadku. Při tom přijat byl poměr nejčastěji se naskytující.

Při 27 cent. šířky na prsou jest 10 cent. š zadku a 9—10 ct. š. slabin			11		10—11
" 30	"	"	12	"	11—12
" 32	"	"	13	"	12—13
" 35	"	"	14	"	12½—13½
" 38	"	"	15	"	13—14
" 40	"	"	16	"	13½—14½
" 42	"	"	17	"	14—15
" 45	"	"	18	"	15—16
" 48	"	"	19	"	16—17
" 50	"	"	20	"	17—18
" 52	"	"	20½	"	18—19
" 54	"	"	21	"	19—20
" 56	"	"	21½	"	20—21
" 58	"	"	22	"	21—22
" 61	"	"	23	"	24—25
" 64	"	"	24	"	25—26

při čemž vzhledem k šířkám zadku přijat obyčejný prostřední poměr; nezat tudíž ohled na to, že při nynejším moderním střihu bére se zadek jeste o ½—1 cent. širší.

Z tabulky této jest ostatně patrno, že se šířka slabin při všech šířkách na prsou až po 54 centimetrů obnáší vždy méně nežli šířka zadku; od 56 cent. šířky na prsou až jest skoro totáž a při 58 až 60 jest již větší. Avšak jak již praveno, mohla by se zde vyskytnouti též o 2 až 1 centimetry menší šířka slabin, jakmile by život ten byl kyčli v těchto tlustých centimetrech v šířce na prsou byla méně značná a tudíž život lépe vyvinut a prohnut. U tlustých mužů s velmi značnou šířkou nad kyčli, může — k ostatně naskytnouti ještě větší šířky a délky nezli při udavu v předcházející tabulce, následkem čehož číslice centimetrů u télomerného pasu nejdou pouze po 25, nýbrž hned až ku předu dále.

Po přikládání následujících měr poprsí platí vždy nejhořejší na slabinách ležící hrana až ku palce širokého tělomerného pasu.

Míra č. 12. Zadní poprsí.

Důležitá tato míra počíná nahoře u obratle šijového, jde odtud svisle přes lopatku až k centrálnímu bodu na spodu nad slabinou, kde končí šířka slabin. Nutno připomenouti, že přední poprsí na tomtéž místě končí. Následkem …

toho poskytují tyto dvě nej … i úplněm vyzkoumání drž … vždy dle tohoto držení nále … ulovíme. Nedostatí, aby se … těchto měr dalo vždy jiné p … mira předního poprsí k po …

Při zcela přímém vzrůstu metrů více nežli zadní poprsí … nežli neprodloužený život, 44 cent. na délku života.

Naproti tomu jest přední délka (bez prodloužení) pravidelně o 4 centimetry větší nežli zadní poprsí, tak že na ono případné by výše uvedeném příkladu 54 centimetrů. Mezi délkou života a přední délkou jest tedy rozdíl 14 cent., kolikero přední poprsí o 10. velké obrneni o 20 a výše plece o 48 centimetrů větší jest, což ovšem zajistí muže jen o přímém vzrůstu. Zcela jiným jest však poměr ten, jakmile držení těla jest nakloněno ku předu nebo na zad promznuto.

K odstranění nedorozumění nutno zde výslovně podotknouti, že při všech délkách těla vzhledem k tomuto poměrům mer rozumejí se vždy skutečné centimetry, nikoli tedy snad části převodní míry, poněvadž všechny míry brány jsou dle obyčejné mírku centimetrové a takové se vypočítávají se.

Musíme vypočítávati tyto míry při slabších a silnějších jakož i při vetších a menších osobách vzdy též o něco jinak. Shledáme tudíž i při střihu přirozené velikosti po 45 centimetrů, polovice šířky na prsou jest 45½ centimetrů zadního poprsí a 50 předního poprsí 41 centimetrech neprodlouženého života, což označuje prostředně, pěkné rostlého, avšak ne příliš velikého muže.

Dále musno připomenouti, že přední poprsí v porovnání se zadním poprsím není též při úplně vzrostlých osob a 5 centimetrů větší, nýbrž vůbec jen v prostředních až po nejsiršší šířky na prsou. Naproti tomu jest u poslednějších již poměr mezi délkou života a zadním poprsím poněkud jiný, poněvadž v poměru k životu bývá poměrně tím větší, čím tlustší jest muž, tak že na př. při 61 centimetrech šířky na prsou, jsou míry tyto: život 48, zadní poprsí 57, přední poprsí 62, přední délka 72 až 74, vždy dle tlouštky břicha. Uvedené zde poznámky nasi prozatím dostatečně k pochopení důležitosti této míry.

(Pokračování.)

Míra č. 13. Přední poprsí.

Když jsme byli změřili zadní poprsí od obratle šijového v rovné čáře souvrž přes pravou lopatku až po vícekráte již jmenovaný centrální bod na pravé slabině, přidržíme hoření konce míry v švu limcovému na obratli šijovém, přeloženou míru pravou rukou přes plece zákazníkovu napřed a když pak tam visí, vedeme pravou rukou mezi pravým ramenem zákazníkovým ze zadu, abychom míru mohli uchopiti; po té i trochu přitahnem a přiložme na tomtéž bod nad slabinou, kde dříve končilo zadní poprsí, tudíž na centrální bod, aneb obdržíme velmi snadno pravé přední poprsí.

Ruka zákazníkova musí vždy zcela kolmo viseti dolů a nesmí si dávati jiné položení, poněvadž by se tím měření měr poprsích stalo nejistým. Pevnější přitahování míry jest při braní míry nutné, protože míra béře se přes kabát a míra přítažena se ještě pevnějí, hlavně když i kabát na plecích vyssátněn. Při tomto přitažením však musíme dbáti, abychom tím nutru nahoře od obratle šijového neztahli, tím kdyby se ramenu mohlo státi, kdybychom ji na onom místě pevně nedrželi.

(Pokračování.)

Ohlášení.

Pánům krejčím!

Upozorňuji pány krejčí, zvlášt z venkova, že mám nyní vždy výborně … stroje za ceny poměrně ta cka d ve – jsem v nejlepsim … s obchodu spojení. Proto necht páni krejčí, kteří sobě nový stroj … jati hodlají, bezprostředně na mne, aneb jim spodu uvedený … návod k – di.

Vojta Čihař,
redaktor "Zlatého dna".

Předplatné
na "Nové Pařížské Mody" se všemi přílohami obnáší:

v Rakousko-Uherském mocnářství a v Bosně čtvrtletně K 3.—, poštou K 3.12, půlletně K 6.—, pošt. K 6.24, celoročně K 12.—, poštou K 12.48. Do Německa, Černé Hory a Srbska i s pošt. zásylkou čtvrtletně K 3.60. Do Ruska, ostatních států Evropy a Ameriky čtvrtletně K 4.—.

Předpláceti možno v každém knihkupectví, zejména v administraci naší v nakladatelství

ALOISA HYNKA
v Praze,
Celetná ulice č. 11 n.

magazines based their illustrations on the French, German and Austrian magazines. The first records of original Czech fashion production did not appear until about the 1920's. Far better results as regards originality were achieved by the fashion papers for men, which occasionally also published some models for women. In the period that we are talking about the last volumes of "Zlaté dno" (The Golden Bottom) appeared. This magazine was published by Vojtěch Čihař between 1862 and 1874. He published not only his own designs, but also those of other famous Prague tailors such as Mr Václav Huttar, Mr Vendelín Mottl and others, and also the designs of tailors from all over the Bohemia. His respectable follower became "Evropské Mody" magazine (The European Fashion), the magazine for cultivating the fashion and professional knowledge which was issued between 1882 and 1898 in Prague and was edited by J. Michalík. This magazine was awarded an honorable prize from the C.K. Ministry in 1891. Besides the above-mentioned men's "Akademické Modní Listy", issued by Karel Vačlena and the Kratinas, some German magazines existed, published in Brno, as well as many worker-oriented fashion papers[60].

Číslo 16. Ročník III.

Damský Modní Obzor

Podzim 1913.

Damský
MODNÍ OBZOR
rodinný illustrovaný časopis paní a dívek českých, věnovaný modě a poučení.

Hlavní spolupracovníci v Paříži, Berlíně, Lipsku a v Praze.

Vydavatel a nakladatel
JAN KRATINA
Praha I.-463,
Melantrichova ul. čís. 15.

Redakce a administrace
Praha I.-463,
Melantrichova ul. čís. 15.

Nefrankované reklamace přijímají se pouze do 8 dnů.

Rukopisy se nevracejí.

TELEFON Č. 423/VIII.
POŠTOVNÍ SPOŘ. Č. 94.282

Damský
MODNÍ OBZOR
vychází čtvrtletně s přílohami:
Dětské mody, Ruční práce, poučnou a střihovou přílohou.

Čísla vycházejí:

Jarní . . . 20. března.
Letní . . . 20. května.
Podzimní . 20. září.
Zimní . . 20. listopadu.

Předplatné na celý rok
K 6·—.

Celoroční předplatitelé obdrží velmi krásné „BLŮZOVÉ ALBUM" úplně zdarma.

Jednotlivé číslo se všemi přílohami K 1·50.

Kdo si zaslané číslo ponechá, považován jest za odběratele.

KRATINOVA „PRVNÍ MODNÍ AKADEMIE KREJČOVSKÁ" V PRAZE,
jest v král. Českém největší a nejoblíbenější ústav, v kterémž jedině možno nabýti nejdokonalejšího odborného vzdělání a vyučití se všem nejmodernějším dámským střihům dle osvědčené Kratinovy soustavy centimetrové. Soustava tato jest uznána za nejlepší a vyznamenána mnoha čestnými cenami.
Kursy počínají se každého 1. a 15. v měsíci. Do kursů rychlých možno nastoupiti každé pondělí. Vyučovací prospekty zdarma a franko.

Adresovati račte:
Kratinova „První Modní Akademie krejč." v Praze I., Melantrichova ul. 15, maj. Jan Kratina.

V tomtéž domě nachází se velkoobchod damským suknem pro konfekce a moderními látkami vůbec JOACHIM WEDELES SYN.

Czech woman and fashion

Historical sources provide us with controversial information about the relationship of Czech middle-class women toward fashion. In "Ženské Listy" (The Women's Papers) from 1878 its editor Mrs Bětka Rozmarná criticises the fashion magazines which "by publishing quickly changing fashion excesses encourages merely dolly birds, cheapen good taste and ruin the sense of economy, raise the desire for rapidly changing luxury and fill the boredom of slothful lifestyle with trifles."

Instead, they called for magazines to meet the needs of a broader audience, by including fashion patterns with wise moderation which would be proper for alteration and sewing at home, and with useful household knowledge and instructions attached to promote education and actually elevate family and social life.[61]

At the same time women's vanity was mocked by Jan Neruda, who, e.g. in his feature column called "To Sweet Little Tyna" written in 1884, depicts the destiny of his young cousin who left for her summer house with the illusion that she would be devoting herself to a farmer's wife household, but soon after her arrival she started to overwhelm her cousin with demands for new dresses and home dresses, because the Prague ladies, who were spending their time at their summer house as well, changed their clothes and housecoats five times a day as if they were at the spa. Neruda, because of little Tyna, was examining the latest fashion, but was at a loss because that summer there existed not three types of fashion as usual, but a hundred - a different one for each lady. So little Tyna could have worn on her head whatever she wanted - a bread basket turned upside down, a guard's box tied under the chin, a straw or silk sledge toppled over, tiny straw replicas of the kitchen sink - that year everything had become a hat. And besides that - all the historical forms: a knight's hat, the "čikoš" hat, everything. "And what decoration should she put on the hat? Half pound of marellos? Or a poetically arranged flowerbed of tiny flowers? Three meters of coarse cotton cut into stripes - put it on, my darling - it's modern! But the most important were the laced bodices - in Bohemia girl's nice bodices had always been much attended to".[62]

The Prague ladies in their summer homes always considered foreign female visitors as their models. "Pařížské Mody" reported in August 1894 that each of the ladies visiting the Karlovy Vary spas had changed at least 80 robes during their six week stay and the same amount of mantles. However, from the same source we could also hear a skeptical voice. In April 1894 the editors promised their readers a report on the most elegant clothes of the female visitors of the Chuchle horse races, but they were unable to fulfil their promise - there were no extraordinary robes at all.[63]

"Český Svět" (The Czech World) magazine founded in 1904 devoted a great deal of its content to the promotion of Czech trade and culture as well as the beauty and elegance of Czech women. "Watch a Prague beauty at a promenade! You well soon discover that the subtle grace of a modern woman is not based only on a delicate aristocratic smile. All the enticing moves will join into a certain harmony of gestures, which make the figure lovely.... our women give Prague its metropolitan character"[64] thus the magazine praised Prague women. It also illustrated several issues with photographic portraits of beautiful Prague women. And so that none could blame the magazine for uncritical acceptance, it proved its standpoint by quoting some French visitors to Prague. The most corteous opinion of those was expressed, although not in the magazine itself, by Auguste Rodin during his stay in Prague in 1902: "The aristocratic beauty of Prague women, their robes and gait ablazed with colour, so graceful and elegant..."[65]

Now let us consider the changes in fashion as they are shown both in the fashion magazines and the preserved artefacts of the collections of the Museum of Decorative Arts in Prague.

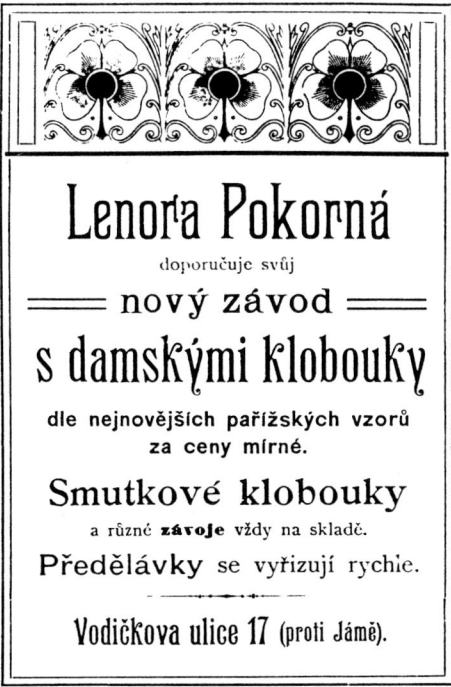

CHANGES IN FASHION LINES BETWEEN 1870 AND 1914

The changes in fashion lines between 1870 and 1914 were determined by aesthetical princip, which also influenced all other kinds of decorative art - historicism.

We came across various forms of historicism in the first part of our exhibition. The historical styles of late classicism and Empire were based on a thorough knowledge of Antique ideas. Designs of national costume from the period around 1848 expressed patriotic feeling and political ambitions and summarised Bohemian fashion before the battle at "Bílá Hora" in 1620. Fashion of the second rococo was also based on an affinity of ideas - its decorativeness and playfulness were expressed in a return to crinoline, the cut of the bodice with long sharp pointed waistline and an abundance of lace and flounces in wide sleeves.

The tendency to take inspiration from historical styles continued after 1870. At the beginning, the style of the period was influenced by the fashion of rococo, which was manifested in the creation of the new polonaise on the skirt and also by the first wave of classicist fashion, which spread from France after 1865. Fashion magazines published fichu called "Marie Antoinette" and paletots in the style of "directoire". As with other branches of art, fashion was also influenced by neo-renaissance and neobaroque. Fashion silhouettes and styles, which resembled the fashion of Renaissance, baroque and rococo, were based on similarities to the style of "Valois" (1328 - 1498), the style of Louis XIII (1610 - 1643), Louis XIV (1643 - 1715) and Louis XV (1715 - 1774). The World Exhibition in Paris in 1889, which took place in the year of the 100th anniversary of the fall of the Bastille[66/], prompted new interest in the period of Louis XVI and styles of "directoire" and Empire. The fichu "Marie Antoinette" appeared again as well as a folded cloak of the

č. 2. Oblek do společnosti. Pohled ze zadu. (K č. 1.)
Střih na přední straně přílohy střihové č. fl., fig. 7. až 11.

Bazar 1870, p. 171.

Bazar > 1892, p. 57.

Módní obzírka.

opět v nastávající sésoně k látkám s mdlým vne jsou krep čínský, bengalin a jiné látky i miláčky, jedná-li se o zhotovení modní zhotovovati oblek ze dvou rozdílných látek, via a hedvábné látky, z krepu a plišu buď nebo souladných, poskytuje variaci velice terá je hodna povšimnutí. Mezi bílými látté vroubkované a žebérkované i zrnkované obení šatů z nich se užívá barevné stuhy aksamitky, která ve více rovných čarách velice pěkný; leč dámy pokročilejšího věku necht se ho vystříhají všemožně. V Paříži, jak doslýcháme, ozdobují dámy obleky bílými krajkami a jako kouzelným proutkem vylouzené objevily se pojednou jako náprsenky vložky, manžety, rukávy, podliny, fiší, povějky a vsazené půle krajkové v sukních; kdo jest majitelkou drahocenných krajek, vytasí se jimi a honosí se jimi na pěkně ozdobené toilety jarní. Záhyby „Watteau" budeme viděti i na šatech letních z fuláru, z muselinu, z hedvábné látky a na šatech z látek krajkových. Záhyby „Watteau" vyžadují vzrůstu úplně ne-úhonného a není radno každé dámě sáhr modě. Ostatně není věcí snadnou udati, dámě vzhledem ku střihu nejlépe svědčúsudek estetický při tom rozhodují. Něk lépe plné tvary, jiná opět lépe se presosoba; nutno na každý způsob studovati a rysy svého těla a hleděti pořdy, aby vynik a zahaleno bylo, co je méně hezké. Šť každá, která v ohledu tvarů tělesných nemu: přílišnou tělnatost, ani na přílišnou hube

Čís. 1. Oblek k vycházkám (ve slohu Jindřicha XI.). Vysv. na přední str. příl.

Čís. 2. Oblek se svrchním šatem (kaftánek) dle ruského střihu. Vysv. na přední str. příl.

Bazar 1894, p. 87.

same name. The style of Empire was identified with the Empress Maria Louise. At the same time, the style of Charles X (1824 - 1830) was popular from 1889. It predominated after 1890 and later it was followed by the fashion of the 1840's and the 1850's. However, features reminiscent of older fashion styles were presented during the 1890's as revealed by the popular "medici" collar, a sash in the style of Louis XV or blouses and bodices in the styles of Louis XIII and Louis XIV. Contemporaries thought that "fashion fin de siècle is a genuine expression of our time. Its characteristic features, allusions to past times and style periods, create an interesting and bright picture, which could hardly be compared to any other."[67] This opinion reveals that the style of historicism was deliberately maintained also in fashion production. However, "Bazar" admitted in another issue that "although new fashion keenly imitates costumes from the past times, everything is stylized and presented in a modern way".[68] The reverse side to historicism was a tendency to create new functional dress. This tendency was closely connected with English fashion style already dating from the period of classicism. The simplicity, purposefulness and firmness of English fashion was praised by Just Bertuch in the magazine "Journal des Luxus und der Moden" in Leipzig in 1786. The same appreciation could be found in the Prague fashion magazine "Mode-Fabrik-und Gewerbszeitung" in 1787 - 1788.[69] After the anglo-mania of classicism and early Empire, the English influence on women's fashion declined and lost ground for several decades. It was not until around 1890 that the competition between English and French fashion styles was mentioned in fashion reviews.[70] In 1893, Bazar magazine stated that fashion had ceased to be controlled purely by French dictate and that English and American fashion patterns were starting to be applied. German ladies selected subdued dresses and Slavic ladies admired the inspiration to be found in Russian, Moravian and Serbian national costumes.[71] English fashion found wider application in connection with the increasing emancipation of women, their involvement in the working process and the development of sporting activities. In the 1890's, "Bazar" magazine, which was orientated

Čís. 37. Šaty s paletkem dle slohu direktorního.
Vysv. na přední str. příl.

towards practical Central-European women, regularly published "tailor-made" dresses, described as "sound with sleeves as simple as on gentlemen's coats".[72/] It also published "English dress for travelling with paletot". In addition to skirt, coat and waistcoat, this dress also contained a blouse and formed a type of clothes which, in "Modní Svět" (Fashion World) magazine, was regarded as "suit" already in 1893.

In this period the types of dresses continued to differ. A blouse and skirt together started to be commonly used as a dress. In the 1860's, this kind of dress found its application not only in fashion abroad, but also in Czech fashion, in which it represented, together with a bolero, a kind of national dress. In the 1890's, a blouse and skirt were used as a dress for walking, sport and also for some formal occasions. They gained great popularity amongst employed women and also amongst the less-wealthy classes, because "blouses had the advantage that it is possible to wear them in combination with older skirts and thus make variations of the dress".[73/]

Tendencies towards purposeful dressing were closely connected with the development of sport and physical activities. In the 1870's and the 1880's designs of dresses for sport seldom appeared in fashion magazines. Most of those, that were published, were dresses for sports that did not demand any special wear, such as skating and roller-skating. Special dresses included riding habits, training suits and swimming suits.

Swimming suits did not change much during the second half of the 19th century. Ladies were mostly carefully covered up, a tight-fitting bodice was worn on the corset, long trousers were gradually shortened, although they were complemented with white or black stockings from ankle to knee and sleeves were also shortened. The swimming suit also included cloth shoes with high laces and straw sole. Dresses were made from red, black or blue cloth, lustre, serge or silk decorated with an abundance of ribbons, ruches and frills. Hair was covered with a bulky cap made of waxed cloth. The reformistic struggle proceeded very slowly. In the first decade of the 20th century, only very brave women dared to wear tricot

Čís. 74. Šaty „Tailor-made" s líčkovou okrasou.
Pohled ze zadu jakož i střih a vyšv. na zadní str. příl.
Čís. XI. Fig. 48—57.

Bazar 1892, p. 118.

Bazar 1895, p. 84.

swimming suits. However, tricot swimming suits became more common after 1910 as documented in issues of "Český Svět" and "Damské Akademické Modní Listy" from 1911. The variety of dresses for sport offered in fashion magazines widened at the beginning of the 1890's. Dresses appeared for lacrosse, lawn-tennis, mountaineering, rowing, hunting and, above all, for cycling. Later, at the beginning of the 20th century, this was enriched with skiing and automobilism.

Dresses for lawn-tennis, lacrosse and rowing had simple fashionable cuts with certain typical details such as a sailor collar with tie and sets imitating men's collars with cuffs. These dresses were made up from light wool materials such as cheviot or flannel with patterns of stripes or squares.

Travelling to the mountains demanded a special kind of wear, which was mostly made from loden cloth and decorated with various applications and leather braiding. Mountain dresses included a half-length skirt worn over trousers made from the same cloth, a blouse made from flannel, cloth or batiste and a half-length loose mantle. The skirt could be tucked up with the aid of buckles and buttons. Women started to exercise by cycling after the introduction of the low bicycle with chain gear. The first races in which Czech women took part were in Baden near Vienna and in Brno in 1893, and later in Ohrada in Prague in 1894. Ladies wore elegant suits, consisting of a short gathered skirt, wide Turkish trousers, loose blouse and coquettish cap. The dress of Miss Titěrová was made from red plush, the dress of Miss Fišerová was white and Miss Kindersteigerová from Zábřeh wore blue.[74/] However, the introduction of dresses for cycling met with certain difficulties - Czech ladies were not too enthusiastic about a pair of trousers, which was common elsewhere. In 1894, the fashion magazine "Pařížské Mody" mentioned a competition between two groups of ladies in Stromovka park in Prague - each group promoted a different style of cycling dress - one wore trousers and the other a skirt. A compromise appeared a year later, when at the ceremony race of the Exhibition of Etnography ladies wore divided

Čís. 49. Šaty s vestou a kabátkem, určené na cesty.
Střih a vysv. na přední str. příl. Čís. I. Fig. 1—10.

BAZAR [K Světozoru č. 30. 1895.]

očka toho řádku se protáhnou společně. — 3. až 7. řádek vzorový: týmže způsobem jako předešlé vzorové řádky, avšak ve 3. vzorovém řádku nabere se místo posledních 8 oček pouze 6 oček, ve 4. vzorovém řádku pouze 4 očka, v 5. vzorovém řádku naberou se 3 očka z posledních 3 začátečních oček a 1 očko na poslední pevné řetízkové očko prostředního základu, v 6. a 7. vzorovém řádku nabere se naproti tomu na konci každého tamojdoucího řádku vždy 1 očko na očko základu, jehož se bylo posledně užilo, pak 1 očko z následujícího očka základu a na začátku zpátečně jdoucího řádku protáhnou se obě tato očka společně (obě protáhnutá očka pokládají se vždy za 1 očko); kromě toho nutno bráti ohled v těchto řádcích, aby se smyčky střídaly týmže způsobem jako dříve. — Následující prouzek pracuje se muškovým vzorem, jak následuje. 1. řádek vzorový: jednotlivou nití z bílé vlny tamojdoucí 1 očko naber vždy z předních 26 kolmých očkových článků posledního vzorového řádku předešlého pruhu, pak 1 očko naber z následujícího očka základu; nazpět, nejbližší 2 očka se protáhnou společně, veškerá ostatní očka protáhnou se za sebou. — 2. řádek vzorový: jednu nit modobarevné vlny, přiberme 5 řetízkových oček. 4 očka, jež se vytáhnou vždy na 1½ cm do délky, naberme ze 4. až 1. řetízkových oček a 3 očka naberme ze zadních kolmých článků nejbližších 3 oček posledního vzorového řádku, při čemž se 1. očko z nich vy-

Čís. 26. Živůtek k obleku čis. 28.

nechá, veškerá očka na háklici protáhnou se 1 očkem a sdrhnou dohromady, pak * 3 řetízková očka, 2 očka naber z 2. a 1. řetízkového očka, 1 očko ze článku nad provléknutým očkem, 1 očko ze zadního článku posledního očka, jež se bylo posledně nabralo, a 3 očka ze zadních kolmých článků nejbližších 3 oček naber, veškerá očka se protáhnou a sdrhnou dohromady, pak se opakuje 7krát od *, avšak v posledním opakování naberou se 2 poslední očka z krajního očka základu, jehož se bylo naposledy užilo a pak z nejbližšího očka základu; posléze 1 pevné řetízkové očko na krajní očka, jež následují, a nit se připevní. — 3 řádek vzorový: bílou vlnou semojdoucí 1 očko z vynechaného řetízkového očka 1. mušky naber, * 1 očko ze řetízkového očka, kterým se byla sdrhla muška a 2 očka z krajních oček nejbližší mušky naber, pak pracujme opakujíc vždy od * týmže způsobem ještě 22 oček a posléze 1 očko z následujícího očka základu naber; nazpět pracuje se jako při 1. vzorovém řádku téhož pruhu. — Oba tyto pruhy opakují se ještě 8krát, avšak pro narudlohnědé pruhy odpadnou začáteční řetízková očka a ke zhotovení pruhu naberou se ze zadních kolmých článků posledního vzorového řádku světlého pruhu, a to nabere se v 1. vzorovém řádku místo 4 oček 5 oček. — Jsou-li pruhy hotovy, spojí se poslední a první pruh sdrhnuvše vždy jeden z předních kolmých článků narudlohnědého pruhu s jedním zadním kolmým článkem světlého

Čís. 27. Oblek ze seržoviny, určený k veslařskému sportu.
Střih a vysv. na zadní str. příl. Čís. XIII. Fig. 71—74.

Čís. 28. Oblek pro dámy k jízdě na dvoukolce.
(K tomu čís. 26.) Střih a vysv. na přední str. příl. Čís. I. Fig. 1—10.

Čís. 29. Oblek pro cestovatelky.
Střih a vysv. na přední str. příl. Čís. IV. Fig. 29—33.

90　　　　　　　　　　　　　　　　B A Z A R.　　　　　　　　　　[Ke Květům č. 24. 1871.]

a spojivši očka do kruhu uháčkuj pak do každého začátečného očka 1 sloupek. Na místo prvního sloupku uháčkuj 3 řetízková očka, za každým sloupkem uháčkuj 2 řetízková očka. 2. řádek: 1 sloupek na každé očko z prvního řádku. Konečně naber z každého očka druhého řádku 2 smyčky a uháčkuj za každou smyčkou 1 řetízkové očko, načež se smyčka na háčku vytáhne v délce as 6 centimt. Je-li kolem růžice řádek smyček dohotoven, zapošij nit a ustřihni ji. Nyní začni z temnější vlny 12 oček a spojivší očka ta do kruhu, uháčkuj na 2 řádky krátkých oček, v nichž přidávej tak, aby ploška háčkovaná se nekrčila. Nyní shotov kolem ještě dlouhý řádek smyček pro třepení. Teď obháčkuj lepenkový kruh, jenž musí býti tak velký, aby se vešel dobře do části z krátkých oček u temnější růžice a sice bledohnědou vlnou, provlikni šňůrové as 6 centimt. dlouhé konce smyčky přední kroužkem světlohnědou vlnou obšitým, pak lepenkovým kruhem a pak skrze obě růžice. Konečně přišij oba konce smyčky u prostřed záhřivadla nahoře několika stehy. Místo trapce dle vyobrazení č. 53. hodí se též trapec dle vyobr. č. 54. Spodní část trapce č. 54. shotoví se ze světlohnědé vlny, jako vlněná bambulka a hlavička se shotoví z lepenky a obšije se též světlohnědou vlnou, načež se povleče sítí z temnohnědé mechovité vlny.

Číslo 57. Vzor k sítkované kulaté pokrývce na stůl.

Usítkuj přední čtvercovitou as 209 dírek dlouhou a rovněž tak širokou část z bílé bavlny neb nití. Bílá místa ve vzoru vyšij bílou bavlnou a temnější místa lesklou přízí, černé kostky zůstanou prázdny. Poslední řádek kostek u obou rovných zevnějších krajů vzoru č. 57. jsou prostředek vzoru. Síť se kolem vyšívané pokrývky vystřihne a zevnější kraj se obšije smyčkovacími stehy, načež se přišije buď třepení neb krajka. Vzor se může též háčkovat neb vyšívat na kanavě. Háčkuje-li se, je

č. 58. Oblek do tělocviku pro dívky od 4 do 6 let.
Střih a vysvětl. na zad. str. příl. střih. č. XII., fig. 30—33.

nice udělej zástřižek pro kapsu podle podvojné čáry, podsaď pak kapesní díl od spodní strany a přistepuj pak příklop podle stejně naznamenaných čísel. Zadek a přednice sešij podle stejných čísel a podsaď pod dolejší kraj kazajky až po tečkovanou čáru na fig. 36. pruh ze svrchu as 4 centimt. široký. Sesadivší límec od 33 do 34 s kazajkou povleč to i s předními cípy přednice až dva centimt. přes tečkovanou čáru od spodní strany pruhovaným drilichem. Podél této čáry ohni přednice a límec k líci. Rukávy ozdob dle částečného naznamenání a sešij je pak od 35 do 36. Dole uvnitř všij do ru-

Číslo 61. Oblek pro hochy od 7 do 9 let.
Střih na zadní straně příl. střih. č. XIII., fig. 34. a 35.

Spodky i halenka obleku toho jsou shotoveny ze šedého plátna a ozdobeny plátěnými pásky a bílými perleťovými knoflíčky. Bílý slaměný klobouk kulatý ozdobí se aksamítem a perem. Střihni halenku dle střihu fig. 34. a 35., rukávy ale přistřihni dle střihu fig. 40., jež náleží k vyobrazení č. 40., však dle potřebné velikosti, pročež je musíš trochu zmenšit. U předního kraje levé přednice přisaď pásek vyobloučený na knoflíkové dírky, jenž je plátěnými pásky ozdoben. Pás k obleku tomu je z černé leštěné kůže.

Číslo 62. Oblek pro hochy od 10 do 12 let.
Střih na zadní straně příl. střih. č. XIV., fig. 36. až 40.

Celý oblek skládá se ze spodků, vesty a kazajky. Spodky a vesta shotoví se z pruhovaného drilichu a kazajka z drilichu hladkého barvy šedé. Okrasy jsou skládané pásky z též látky co oblek. Kulatý buď slaměný neb leštěný klobouk kožený ozdobí se aksamítem a perem kohoutím. Kazajku střihni dle střihu fig. 36. a 40. vždy po dvou dílech, dle fig. 38. a 39. střihni po jednom díle v prostředku v celosti. Příklopy kapesní přistřihni z drilichu pruhovaného dle fig. 37. Do pravé přednice

---

skirts.[75/] Divided skirts for cycling had to be wide enough to enable free movement of the legs and, at the same time, not too wide so as not to blow up during a ride. At the end of the 19th century, another invention appeared - a smooth white, black or checked tricot blouse with roller collar made from Scottish Highland wool, called "a sweater". It was quite supple and tight-fitting and ladies could fasten their coats to the handle bars and wear only a sweater if days were warm.[76/]

As we said in the first part of this catalogue, winter sports were very popular in Bohemia. Starting in the 1870's, skating figures appeared in the fashion magazines. They were comfortable in warm winter coats decorated with fur, warm caps and muffs. Their dresses were not different to contemporary winter fashion dresses, only a shorter skirt implied that they were meant for sport. Women made their way to the mountains much later than men. The first of their dresses were suits and consisted of warm winter coats or mantelets and half-length skirts. After 1910, trousers without a skirt became widely used for skiing sports. Motoring fell somewhere in the middle between sport and purposeful activity. However, it also demanded a special kind of

---

Založeno 1885.
Marie Hájková,
Praha, Ovocný trh č. 19.
Velký výběr dětských šatečků, pláštíčků a žaketů
vlastní výroby,
dle nejnovějších vzorů za ceny nejlevnější.
Velký výběr dětských klobouků a čepečků
dle nejnovějších modelů.

Košile hladké, sámkové, barevné, turistické.
Límce, manžety, kravaty v nevídaném jinde výběru a levných cenách doporučuje
J. Novák, Praha,
Vodičkova ulice „u Štajgrů".

Č. 1. Modrý flanelový oblek koupelní pro hošíka. Vysvětlení na před. str. příl. střih.

Č. 2. Koupelní oblek (spodky a dlouhá halenka) z bile a červeně pruhovaného flanelu. Střih a vysvětlení na přední str. příl. střih. č. II., fig. 5—8.

Č. 3. Oděv ku koupání neb plavání (spodky, krátká halenka a šos) z červeného flanelu. Střih a vysvětlení na přední str. příl. střih. č. III., fig. 9—12.

Č. 4. Bílý flanelový oblek koupelní. Střih a vysvětlení na přední str. příl. střih. č. I., fig. 1—4.

Číslo 1. až 4. Rozličné obleky ke koupání neb plavání.

Bazar 1897, p. 125.

Nové Pařížské Mody 1906, no. 17, p. 3.

wear, especially at the beginning of the era when cars were open-topped. Women's motoring fashion was largely inspired by men's dress, which was then merely enhanced with some elements of women fashion. At the centre of motoring dress was either a heavy raglan overcoat, which served as protection against bad weather, or a coat with mantelet collar, lapels and patch pockets. These coats were made up from unrefined silk, mohair or impregnated cotton cloth. A motoring wrap was also an essential accessory. It was wrapped around the hat and fluttered behind the car. The most typical feature of all sport dresses was a purposeful cut and materials of the best quality. English fabrics were highly recommended, although, as Bazar magazine mentioned in 1897, Czech cloth and other materials are equal in quality to English ones.[77/] Not only English cuts and patterns, but also English taste achieved a great popularity. It must have been the purposefulness and simplicity of sport dresses that struck a reporter of the Bazar magazine who saw the beginning of the development of modern dress in sporting dresses. "We could hardly imagine a bigger difference than the one which exists in contemporary fashion. There is a keen imitation of old historical costumes on the one hand and a new, interesting move towards the future era on the other, whose forerunners seem to be modern sporting suits."[78/]

Obr. 11. Prýmek k ozdobení podzimních šatů.

Obr. 12. Ozdobný prýmek na podzimní šaty.

Popis vyobrazených toilett.

Obr. 1. Podzimní anglický oblek ze sukna s jupičkou empire. K sukni může se oblékati bluza z látky šatů, dle anglického spůsobu upravená, jejíž přední a zadní díly zdobí se jen přištepovanými pásky z látky, aneb bluza, lišící se barvy, z hedvábí, krajek neb jiné vzdušné látky, jako jest mušelín-chiffon neb čínský krep. K zakončení bluzy připíná se pás ze satinové stuhy liberty, ozdobnou sponou provléknutý. Jupička, jak na obr. viděti, několika krátkými švy projmutá, zapíná se jen v hořejší polovině čtyřmi kovovými neb látkou napnutými knoflíky a zdobí v patřičném tvaru stříženými, oboustranně přištepovanými pásky látky, které ohraničují zároveň okraj jupičky. Přehnutý límeček napne se sametem, lišicí se barvy a a výložky hedvábnou látkou, jsou-li tyto jen z látky šatů, pak se proštepují. Malé výložky přehnou se z předních dílů. K polodlouhému, dole užšímu rukávu, pojí se výdutek z taffetu, aneb místo výdutku viděti jest rukáv bluzy. Sukně

Obr. 13. Oblek z himalajského lodenu s jupičkou v tvaru empírovém na hon; střihu jupičky užiti lze dle čís. 7. na dnešní střihové příloze. — Obr. 14. Klobouk z velourové plsti na hon. — Obr. 15. Plášť z anglické vlněné látky k cestování a k jízdě v automobilu; zadní stranu viz obr. 53 ; střihu užiti lze dle čís. 8. na dnešní střihové příloze. — Obr. 16. Klobouk z plsti s ochranným závojem k jízdě v automobilu.

FASHION BETWEEN 1870 and 1876

The year 1870 did not mark any particular turning point in style development. At the end of the sixties we left fashion style at the stage of a moderately raised waist, widened sleeves and the skirts either hitched up into some kind of a modern polonaise, or plain with a train, complemented by separate little tails, pinned on at the waist. The tendency toward great attention to the decoration of the skirt continued in the 1870's. The shape of the skirt was supported by a bustle, made of a horsehair cloth or a wire structure, covered with linen. Although the skirt was still lightly pleated in front, the back attracts our attention because of the different methods of hitching it up using a system of tapes stitched on underneath the skirt, which created a wide, richly arranged drapery. The form of bodices became simpler and by 1872 the waist came back to its natural place again. In the same year the sleeves became consistently fitted. The alternative to short jackets and bodices became bodices with a short back provided with folded tails, but longer in front, with a prolonged, apron-like part, which had prepared the way for the reception of the princess cut. In the following years the type of dress did not change, except that the silhouette somewhat narrowed. The skirt did not lose its decorativeness - over

[Ke Květům č. 32. 1870.]

a hnědým hedbávím. Kolem středu běží kraječek, který se pošívá v obloučkách se zlatou šňůrkou. V každém obloučku je několik stehů zlatou nitkou vyšito. Ostatní části vzoru jsou vyšity štepem z hnědého hedbáví a uzlíčky ze světlo a temnohnědého hedbáví.

Vyšívaný okolek na bíle a šedě pruhovaném drilichu.
K tomu vyobrazení č. 47.

Podobnými okolky roubí se ubrusy, povlikají se polštáře v oknech atd. Vzor vyšij buď s barevným hedbávím, vlnou aneb též bavlnou na drilichu bíle a šedě pruhovaném, chrpy modře, metlice

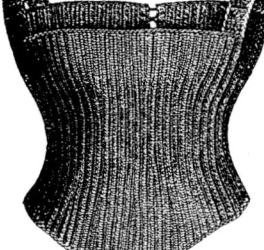

Č. 52. Háčkovaná šněrovačka pro dívky od 8 do 10 let.

Č. 48. Šněrova (K tomu vyobr. stř

Č. 49. Šněrovačka narovnavací pro dívky od 12 do 14 let. Pohled s předu. (K tomu vyobr. č. 50.)
Střih a vysvětlení na zad. str. příl. střih. č. X., fig. 56–63.

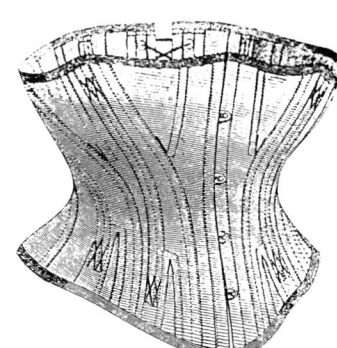

Č. 54. Šněrovačka ze šedého drilichu.
(K tomu vyobr. č. 60., 63. a 64.)
Střih a vysvětl. na před. str. příl. střih. č. V.,

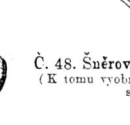

SALON
× × Ste
Praha-II., S

Č. 58. Spodnička k šatům s vlečkou.
Střih na zadní str. příl. stř.

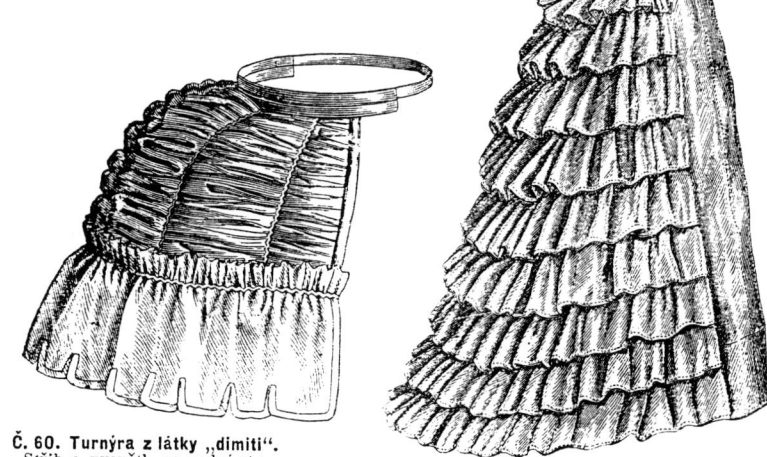

Č. 60. Turnýra z látky „dimiti".
Střih a vysvětl. na zadní str. příl. stř. č. XII, fig. 36 a 37.

Č. 37. Spodnička z dimity pod šaty s vlečkou.

Č. 36.
Střih a vysv
přílohy stř

Bazar
1873, p. 66,
1874, p. 106,
1876, p. 55.

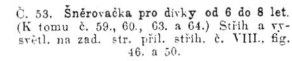

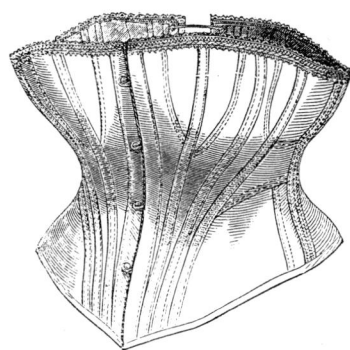

the narrow skirt, extended to make a train, there was a tunic with bowl-shaped or apron-shaped pleats. At the back the tunic was arranged toward the centre and was decorated with ribbons, laces and so on. A substantial change occured after 1875, when the bustle started to move lower to under the waist. This enabled an extension of the bodices - they became very tight and were supported by whalebones. They were either in the form of a jacket with straight bottom hem, reaching under the hips, or they could be of cuirass form. In 1876 the drapery at the back somewhat calmed down and the dresses of the princess cut started to appeared in the magazines. Their length reached down to the ankles and underneath an underskirt was worn. This dress was buttoned lengthwise from the top to the bottom and was decorated with a number of buttons. The clothes preserved in the collection of the Museum of Decorative Arts demonstrate almost all of the above-mentioned types. For casual wear two-piece dresses were very popular with a jacket and a plain skirt, hitched up at the back. This type is represented here by dress inv. no. 39.576 of turquoise blue taffeta, which probably comes from Hořice from between the years 1870 and 1875. It has a plain skirt made of several pieces with ribbons for suspending and a jacket, and is decorated by ruches. The same type of dress is represented by dress inv. no. 82.349 of grey taffeta with blue edging of a similar style. A more intricate type is represented by the violet taffeta dress from between the years

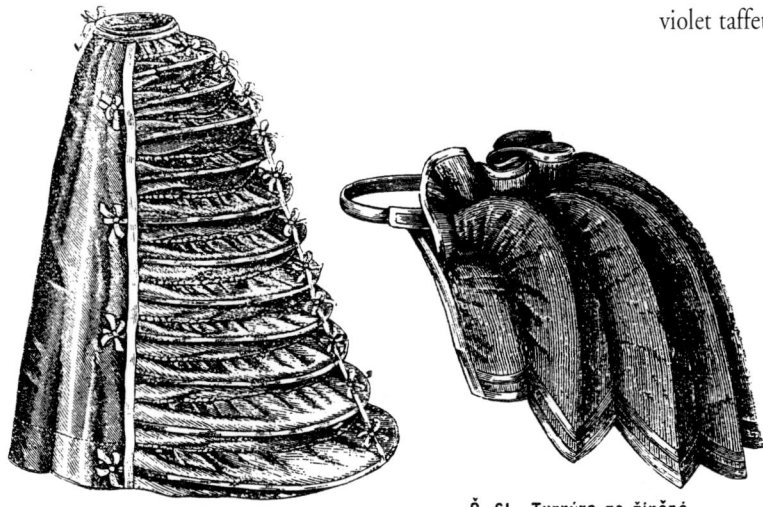

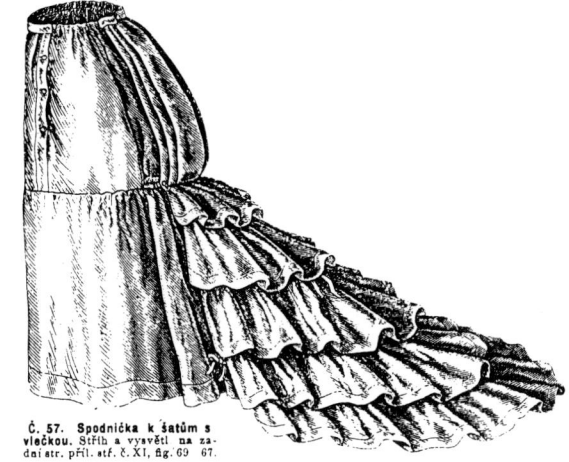

Č. 1. **Cestovní oblek ze srnobarevné látky „mozambique".** Vysvětl. na přední str. příl. stř.
Č. 2. **Cestovní oblek ze šedého mohéru.** Vysvětl. na přední str. příl. stř.
Č. 3. **Oblek pro dívky od 6 do 8 let.** Vysvětl. na přední str. příl. stř.
Č. 4. **Cestovní oblek z přížloutlé „toile-de-soie".** Střih a vysvětl. na přední str. příl. stř. č. 1, fig. 1—7.
Č. 5. **Cestovní oblek z „foulard-japonais".** Střih a vysvětl. na přední str. příl. stř. č. II, fig. 8 a 9.

Č. 1—5. Cestovní obleky pro dámy a děti.

1872 and 1874 inv. no. 91.477 with velvet edgings of the same colour and a segmented skirt with a train, over which was worn a dress of coat-form in front and a tunic with short little tails at the back. The dress belonged to a distiller's wife from Hradec Králové. The grey taffeta dress inv. no. 37.269 is of a princess cut. It was worn over an underskirt. The front piece is full-length buttoned up with two rows of buttons, the back piece is plain, not arranged, decorated with lace hems and buttons. If we consider the fact that the drapery was less flamboyant and if we evaluate the kind of decoration, we can place this dress somewhere between the years 1876 and 1877. In contrast to the narrow silhouette of the skirt of this period, as shown in the fashion papers, the skirt of this dress still keeps its conservative width.

Housecoats represent a special type, for example the dressing gown, which was the predecessor of the "tea-gown". The exhibit inv. no. 96.846 in the collection of the Museum of Decorative Arts has the princess cut with a train and is decorated with trios of buttons near the oblique buttoning. A very close analogy to this dress is shown in an illustration in "Bazar" from 9 January 1877.

Bazar
1874,
p. 85.

Bazar 1871, p. 16.

Bazar 1876.

Dámské klobouky

elegantní doporučuje **Josefa Houdková, PRAHA-I.**,
Malé náměstí 143 vedle firmy Rott.
Opravy se rychle vyřizují.

Č. 62. Spodní sukně z diagonální látky.
Střih viz vysvětl. na zadní str. příl. str.

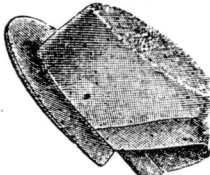

Č. 57. Podstavec ku klobouku č. 27.

Č. 64. Vázanka k nákrčníku, zhotovená z tylu, krajek a grogrénky.

Č. 63. Spodní sukně ze serge. Střih a vysvětl. na zadní str. příl. str. č. IX, fig. 29—31.

Č. 63. Oblek soukenný. Vysvětl. na zadní str. příl. stř.

Č. 64 Oblek zhotovený z pruhované a jednobarevné látky vigoňské. Pohled na přední stranu. (K tomu č. 49.) Střih a vysvětl. na zadní str. příl. stř. č. VII, fig. 32ab—46.

Č. 65. Oblek z pruhované a jednobarevné látky chevlotu. Pohled na zadní stranu. (K tomu č. 48.) Vysvětl. na zadní str. příl. stř.

Č. 86. Šaty zhotovené z látky „Bure" a paletko z látky „drap-Melbourne". Vysvětl. na zadní str. příl. stř.

Č. 63—66. Oděvy ženské ku klouzání.

Canfieldova **potítka.**
Beze švů   Bez zápachu
Nepromokavé
Nedostižitelný ochranný prostředek do šatů.
Canfield Rubber Co.,
Hamburk, Grosse Bleichen 16.
Pravá pouze, jsou-li opatřená známkou „Canfield".
Každému potítku připojen jest záruční list.

Bazar 1877, p. 8.

Fashion between 1870 and 1876

Dress of violet taffeta with one-colour edging.
Bohemia 1872 - 1874, inv. no. 91.477.

Bazar 1877, p. 7.
Reverse side
of the picture on page 56.

FASHION BETWEEN 1877 and 1881

Fashion in the late 1870's and beginning of the 1880's further developed the tendencies of the period before. The silhouette became tighter and of a sheath cut, the bustle moved lower to under the waist. The bodices were tight and extended, especially at the back where the tails of the back pieces came lower under the hips and covered the draperies of the skirt. The tube cut skirt was covered in front by various decorations such as flounces, frills, ruches and puffed and gathered bands. Another variation was represented by the application of folded pieces or a narrow tunic decorated with lace, fringe, tassels or flower festoons on the ball robes. The silhouette of the straight skirt is distorted just above the ground by a narrow strip of fanshaped hems. The skirts for casual wear also had a train at the back which became shorter from 1879 and almost disappeared in 1881. This basic type was enriched gradually by tiny innovations. Around 1879 a pannier drapery appeared on the skirts, especially on the dresses with cuirass bodices, which resembled rococo skirts. After 1880 the drapery on the skirt hang down similar to handkerchief tips. During 1881 conspicuous decorations appeared, such as tied stripes of cloth, big bows, tuck-ups right under the waist on the tails of the jacket or on the tips of the bodice. The

Bazar 1880, p. 65.

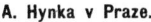

padding under the skirt slowly moved up toward the waist.

A popular type of garment from this period, especially of the outdoor dress type, was a two-piece dress with an extended tight jacket. As for the evening dresses, bodices cut deeply at the hips were still popular.

Outer dresses, of course, followed the fashionable silhouette especially by the cut of their back pieces, which adjusted to the shape of the skirts. The individual pieces varied according to the length of the garment and cut of the sleeves. The longest was a cloak called "Palandrana", made most frequently of cloth, with set-in sleeves. Another type, called "Dolman", was a semi-tight-fitting coat and usually reached down to the hips. Its sleeves were cut at the level of the elbow. Mantelets and capes were even looser and their sleeves had yet more simple form. Paletots were tight-fitting coats, which reached down to the hips. Their style was in fact the same as the style of the jacket of a two-piece dress.

How did the ladies deal with the inspiration provided by fashion magazines? The newspaper reports from balls called "Národní Beseda" (The National Patriotic Meeting) as early as in 1876 praised the female participants saying, that "the robes were all made according to the latest style, the bodices were very tight and so the slimness of the figure was gracefully emphasized". In 1878 the reporter points out the trains, which were too long in his opinion - one of them even longer than three meters. Also in 1879 the robes were mostly very rich, made of silk combined with silver and golden brocade. The reporter depicts the style as being either "princesse" or "à la Maintenon" or with long bodice "à l'anglaise". The trains were still long, arranged artificially and tastefully and the decolletages were moderate. Only when the neckline was more daring, was it

Bazar 1881, p. 121.

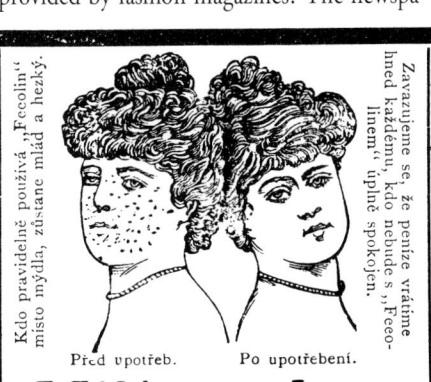

Dress of grey taffeta. Bohemia around 1880, inv. no. 68.887.
Winter coat „dolman". Bohemia around, 1880, inv. no. 68.977.

Woolen checked dress. Bohemia 1881 - 1882, inv. no. 87.987.

covered with lace. Only in 1880 were the trains shortened and in harmony with the small dancing space. In 1881 the reporter highlighted as a novelty the two-colour suits with "armoured" bodices of a different colour.[79]

Unfortunately we do not have any ball robes of this period in our collection, which would be undoubtedly of Czech origin. The only dress in our inventory, inv. no. 70.058, classified as a court robe from the period between the years 1875 and 1880 in white satin combined with white tulle and richly embroidered with silver, is in such a bad shape that it is impossible to do any further research on it. It is also the oldest dress in the collection of the Museum of Decorative Arts marked with a workshop label - the firm was Julie Eisner, Prague. We will learn more about ceremonial garments from the collection of wedding dresses. Their advantage is that they can usually be dated exactly and are more often than the others marked by the author's firm label. The oldest dated dress is the one of white satin inv. no. 89.526 from 1879, which comes from the Betty Beyer workshop in Prague. The dress is not cut in the waist and is decorated on the front piece of the skirt with horizontal stripes of ruches, frills and flounces. The back piece is arranged with a long train. The next dress (inv. no. 73.875) from the period between 1879 and 1880 is a two-piece dress, with a jacket extended under the hips, prolonged at the back into a dull tip above the cascade of drapery of the back piece of the skirt. The front piece of the skirt is covered with the bowl-shaped folds of a tunic. The dress is decorated with beaded embroidery,

Bazar 1880, p. 188.

ruches and braids. It was made in Prague in "Zur schwarzen Mutter Gottes" workshop. A slightly younger dress (inv. no. 50.909) from the Karla Oswald workshop from 1882, is a two-piece dress with a cuirass bodice with lacing at the back and overcasts in front at the waist. The skirt is plain in front, decorated with embroidery and a short pannier drapery which comes out of the bodice toward the back, where it is arranged into cascades. This drapery, which appears in "Bazar" in 1881 can be found also on the next wedding dress inv. no. 73.874, which was probably created in the same period. Their style is similar, the only difference being that the bodice is buttoned in front and the back piece is not cut in the waistline.

Outdoor suits of this period from the collection of the Museum of Decorative Arts also illustrate different types of styles. Dress inv. no. 58.595 of grey taffeta represents the type with cuirass bodice deeply cut on the hips, with a skirt complemented by a tunic with apron-shaped folds in front and cascade-arranged drapery under the tails of the bodice at the back. A very elegant example is provided by the trio of similar two-piece dresses - in grey taffeta, black woollen poplin and wine-red striped damask - with longer jacket and a narrow skirt, arranged in front with tiny ruches or folds (inv. no. 88.627 black, inv. no. 68.887 grey, inv. no. 81.352 red) and with rich drapery at the back. They were created around 1880. A similar dress is the travelling suit made of two chequered woollen materials, inv. no. 87.987, complementary in colour, which have an extended jacket and the skirt decorated in front with stripes of ruches and frills. The handkerchief-like tips at the hips and drapery, situated on the tails of the jacket, classifies this dress into the period between 1881 and 1882.

Č. 38. Aksamitový dolman.
Č. 39. Plášť ze sukna kostkovaného.

Bazar 1882, p. 4-5.

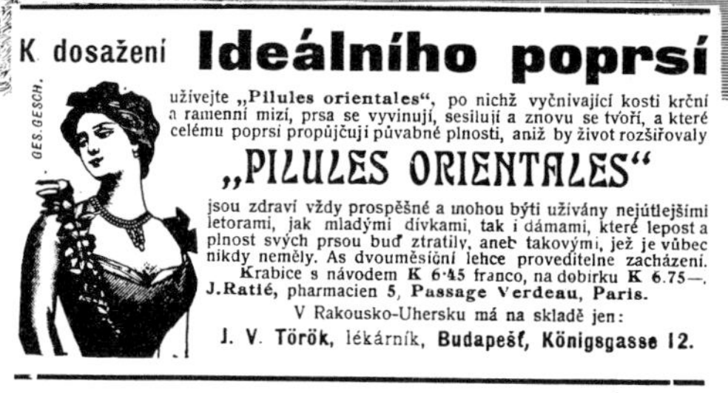

Bazar 1885, p. 119, 1886, p. 96.

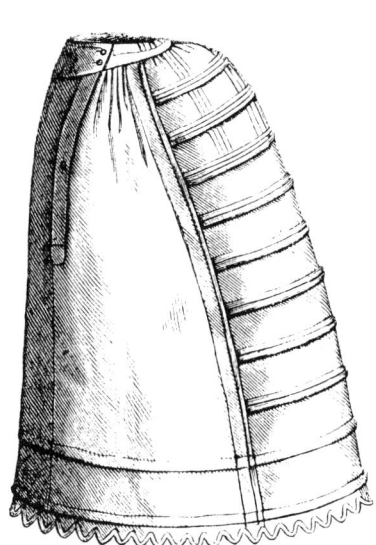

Čís. 38. Krinolina. (K tomu č. 39.)
Střih a vysv. na přední str. příl.,
čís. V., fig. 22–25.

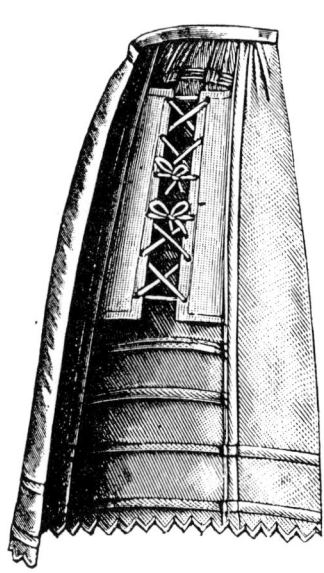

Čís. 39. Zadní půle krinoliny.
Pohl. zevnitř. (K č. 38.) Střih a vysv.
na přední str. příl. Čís. V. Fig 22–25.

Čís. 58. Spodní sukně s turnýrou.
Střih a vysv. na zadní str. příl. Čís. VII.
Fig. 39–41.

A FASHION BETWEEN 1882 and 1888

As we have already noticed, the following change in fashion was already apparent as early as 1881 and, similar to previous years, the determining factor of the whole silhouette had been the shape of skirt. Padding of the bustle, which still remains the substantial construction constituent, started to move toward the waist during 1881 and this move continued in the following years. At the same time the shape of skirt became wider again, but in comparison with the 1870's it was more angular and shorter. In the period between 1882 and 1887 the length of the skirt reaches the ankles. However, eventually the details of the cuts changed - in 1882 the richness of the skirt was achieved by a complex arrangement of the drapery on both the back and front pieces and it was complemented by a lot of decorative material such as lace, voile, bows and embroidered flounces. Further on, the volume of the skirt widened still further and at the same time the arrangement became simpler. In 1884 the skirt had a bulky shape with a simple smooth surface. Pleated frills at the hem of the skirts dissappeared, the cloth flowed down into calm folds and a folded skirt under a tunic became popular. At the same time an asymmetric styling of folds and overlapping of different materials in layers started. This way of decoration was still popular until 1887, when the simplicity of style and material came into fashion again. However, there were still two layers - an underskirt and an arranged tunic over it.

Bazar 1885, p. 36.

During this decade the bodices did not change particularly - they still remained cuirass-cut on the hips or had a jacket shape - they merely became shorter as the bustle moved up to the waist. The points at the waist, still sharp in 1883, became shallow after 1885. A fashion novelty from the beginning of the 1880's was the opening of the bodice in front at the buttoning where a plastron was inserted. The plastron could broaden from the waist or as far as

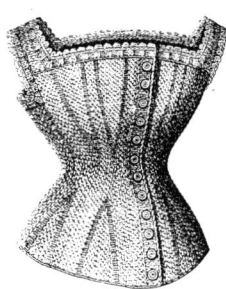

Č. 56. Spodní živůtek ženský.
Pletená a háčkovaná práce.

Čís. 36. Šaty ze vzorkovaného voilu a hedvábné látky.
Vysvětl. na přední straně příl.

Divadelní kukátka
pravá, achromatická od 4 zl. výše, **salonní lorgnety, brejle** a **skřipce** ze zlata, želvy nebo 14kar. doublé od zl. 2·50, **aneroidy, rýsovadla, pedometry, stereoskopy,** fonografy od 9 zl., kapesní fotografické aparáty za 2 zl. 50 kr. a cestovní komory fotografické od zl. 6·— výše dodává se zárukou

Optický závod M. Růžička (F. Durst)
Praha-I., Ovocná ulice č. 2.

Čís. 24 a 25. Klobouk z italského pletmového. Pohled ze předu a zadu

Čís. 28. Šaty z diagonálu.
Přehled střihu tuniky a vysv. na zadní str. příl.

Čís. 29. Šaty z jednobarevné a vzorkované látky.
Vysvětl. na přední str. příl.

2 očka se přeskočí, 7 sloupků na ve 7 oček. * 3 řet. očka. 1 krátké očko n sledující očko. 3 řet. očka. 1 sloupek dlejší sloupek, od * se 4krát opakuje sloupků na 6 sloupků. 3 řet. očka, 1 očko na 3. následující očko. 3 řet. sloupek na 5. následující očko. 3. řádeř oček. 7 sloupků na vedlejších 7 sloupk střídavě 5 řet. oček, 1 sloupek na sloupek, pak 6 sloupků na 6 sloupků 5 řet. oček, 7 oček se přeskočí, 1 slo očko vedle. 4. řádek: jako 2. řád sloupky, které se kladou na sloupky pře řádku, jsou uháčkovány kolem obou 5. řádek: 8 řet. oček, 1 sloupek na sloupek. 5 řet. oček, 1 sloupek na 6 dující očko. 5krát střídavě 5 řet. oček, 1 na vedlejší sloupek, pak 5 sloupků. na 6. následující očko. 5 řet. oček. 1 na 8. očko. 6. řádek: * 5 řet. oček. 1 očko na prostřední z vedlejších 5 řet 3 řet. očka. 1 sloupek na vedlejší slou * se 3krát opakuje; ale při každém vání se uháčkuje místo prvních 5 ře pouze 3 řet. očka, pak následuje 6 slo 6 oček, + 3 řet. očka, 1 krátké očko n sledující očko. 3 řet. očka. 1 sloupek dlejší sloupek, od + se 3krát opakuje dek: 8 řet. oček. 8 oček se přeskočí střídavě 1 sloupek na vedlejší sloupek, oček. pak 7 sloupků na 7 sloupků vedle střídavě 5 řet. oček, 1 sloupek na 5 řet. oček předešlého řádku. 8. řád řet. oček. 1 krátké očko na prostředn dlejších 5 řet. oček. 3 řet. očka, 1 na vedlejší sloupek. od * se 2krát o ale místo prvních 5 řet. oček se uhá řet. očka, pak 18 sloupků na 18 oček ších. + 3 řet. očka, 1 krátké očko na sledující očko. 3 řet. očka, 1 sloupek na s následující, od + 2krát opakuj. 9. řádek oček. 8 oček se přeskočí, 2krát střídavě sloupek na vedlejší sloupek. 5 řet. oček 19 sloupek na 19 sloupků. 3krát střídavě oček. 1 sloupek na sloupek vedle. 10.

< Bazar 1886, p. 44.

the edge of the bodice. It could be made of lace, of a different cloth to the dress or it could be plain or tucked up. The collar was standing and it eventually became higher and higher. It was complemented by a ruche from delicate materials as well as the popular square or oval decoltages of ceremonial dresses. The sleeves started to get shorter in 1882. From 1883 evening dresses and summer dresses had their sleeves short to the elbow in general. Around 1883 the ball robes had short, pipe-shaped sleeves and in the second half of the decade they were equipped merely with narrow shoulder straps with short frills.

In the Museum of Decorative Arts' set from this period there are several interesting pieces of garment which come from Vienna, e.g. an evening ceremonial dress of yellow-green damask and brick-red velvet created in the Hansal workshop, a white ball robe of white satin with rich pink and silver embroidery created by the Varges workshop or a wine-red damask dress created by the workshop of Ant. Suské.

There is an interesting pair of dresses illustrating the historicizing tendencies in fashion - that is dress inv. no. 82.351, in red velvet with short bodice with pointed waistline, with lace plastron with a standing collar and a skirt, into

Dress of slightly violet taffeta and lace. Bohemia around 1885, inv. no. 33.367.

which is inserted a grey corded silk piece with applique roses. This dress was inspired by Renaissance fashion and was created around 1887. The second dress is inv. no. 50.902. Its bodice is made of red plush and violet taffeta and is decorated with a hung bead fringe at the waist. The sleeves are horizontally gathered and folded into a head, and at the back a Watteau-type fold flows down into a train. According to family tradition this dress was made for the ceremonial opening of the National Theatre in 1883, although some of the signs, like the cut of the bodice and the shape of sleeves, classifies the dress as late as towards the end of the 1880's.

se neplete dále. Nyní se zhotoví přednice na očkách mezi zadkovými díly na 48 řádků vysoko úplně hladce a tímže způsobem, jako ostatní v rovném směru nad přidáváním předešlého řádku se jednou přidá a ve středu se jednou ujme, při dávání se však opakuje v 61., 66., 72., 78., 84. a 90. řádku. V posledních dvou řadách se obřetízkují pro ramenka 16 oček a spojí se to s krajními očky dílů zadkových. Teď nabereme krajní očka dílů zadkových na dráty a pleťme najednou úplně hladce, pak ve 2. řádku: očka zadní, příčního kraje úplně hladce, kolem krku řádek dírek, jako v 19. řádku. 3. až 5. řádek: úplně hladce, ale v prvních z těchto řádků se při pravém dílu zadkovém v mezerách 7 oček nechá volnost vždy pro knoflíkovou dírku, jichž jest 5. Pro dírku se níž obtočí kolem drátu a následující 2 očka se upletou hladce dohromady, mimo se krajní očka

Wine-red dress
of silk.
Vienna around 1884,
inv. no. 51.676.
Mantle of black silk.
Prague or Vienna around 1885,
inv. no. 61.776.

Čís. 16. Pletená botka pro děti.

Botka upletena byla z bílé zefirové vlny na prostředních drátech úplně hladce; jen kraj byl vzorkovaný a opatřen řádkem dírek, kterýmiž se gumová stužka provleče a botka pak se vázankou ozdobí. Začněme pléstí od středu podešve na 24 oček a pleťme drátky semo tamo 24krát pořád hladce. S obou stran se ve 2., 4., 6. a 8. řádku pro patu 3. očka od počátku uplete 1 hladce, 1 po anglicku hladce, pak pro špičku botky se na konci každého řádku rovného počtu z třetího předposledního očka podobným způsobem jedno očko přidá. V 25. řádku se uplete prvních 22 oček na zvláštních drátech, na ostatních 18 očkách se plete dolejší část nártová, a sice 32 řádků pořád ve stejném počtu oček. Nyní se započne na 22 očkách znova ve spojení s ostatním a na všech 40 očkách se plete ještě 40 řad, které jsou rovněž

Dress of velvet,
corded silk and lace.
Bohemia around 1887,
inv. no. 82.351.

I. ČESKÁ KUCHYNĚ
renomovaná česká škola kuchařská řízená Ant. Dolýškovou
V PRAZE, VODIČKOVA ULICE č. 33
přijímá slečny k vyučení za nejpříznivějších podmínek.
HOSTINY SVATEBNÍ, SLAVNOSTNÍ
a jiné.
Pochvalná doporučení z nejpřednějších rodin!

Čís. 23. Figarová jupička z perlového tylu.
Střih a vysv. na zadní str. příl. Čís. XIX. Fig. 68—70.

Pěstování květin v domácnosti. Od zkušeného pěstitele květin. Se 48 vyobrazeními. Praktická kniha tato doporučuje se zahradníkům, milovníkům a vůbec pěstitelům květin co nejlépe. Obsah: O prsti či zemi zahradní. Nádoby k pěstění květin. O vodě a zalévání. Provětrávání květin. Rozmnožování květin. O přesazování květin. Obřezávání květin. Přezimování květin. Nepřátelé květin. Seznam květin, které se dají s výhodou v domácnosti pěstovat. Cena 1 K 20 h., poštou (v známkách neb poukázkou) 1 K 30 h.

Bazar
1877,
p. 84.

FASHION BETWEEN 1889 and 1899

In fashions around 1890, some of the characteristic features of the previous period were still used, but gradually they were changed toward a new silhouette. At the beginning the skirt still remained divided into two layers - the underskirt, which was smooth, and the upper skirt, which was arranged into a tunic or apron, but the volume was becoming less. The back piece remained padded with bustle and the folds became stiffer and less segmented depending on the materials used. The most common materials were heavy drapery cloths, cashmere and woollen crepes. Only as late as during 1890 did the skirt lose the tunic. The bodices were often of a waistcoat-style with plastron or in the form of a tight blouse with a high-standing collar and a moderately lowered waist. The sleeves were fitted into deep armholes and were pleated at the top. There was still no apparent substantial change in style, but nevertheless the reporter of "Bazar" noticed in June 1889 that "it seems, that the modistes immediately concentrate their attention on bodices, while, once, the skirts were the main subject of their decorative efforts..."[80/] And the further developments confirmed her words.

Fashion after 1892 resembles the Biedermeier silhouette of an hour-glass. The skirts, straight and smooth since 1890, became broader and broader toward the middle of the decade and changed their cut, so that in 1893 the new fashion became bell skirts and skirts with inserted gores which widened the lower edge, club-shaped skirts, where each piece of the skirt created an arch at the hem, fan-shaped skirts, and later on pleated skirts.

The fashionable silhouette was also achieved by the cut and decorative design of bodices. Jackets and bodices of "bolero", "figaro", "zuave" style, the ones with a plastron or a blouse bodices with lace and ribbon decorations, wide collars and epolettes and ribbons, were designed so that they created wide shoulders.

The most distinctive sign of fashion development became the sleeves.

Šněrovačky
tvaru osvědčeně výtečného v dobré jakosti
při mírných cenách
doporučuje
tovární sklad firmy:
J. NOVAK,
PRAHA, Vodičkova ulice »u Štajgrů«.

é Mody 1893.

Pařížské Mody 1894, p. 376.

Obr. 24. — Nová úprava šněrovaček.

Bazar 1893, s. 165. Čís. 28. Halenka ze satýnu „Merveilleux"
s okrasou krajkovou.
Střih a vysv. na přední str. příl Čís I. Fig. 1—10.

Čís. 29. Batistová halenka s vyšíváním.
Vysv. na přední str. příl.

Čís. 9. Spodní sukně ze vzorkované
hedvábné látky.
Střihový přehled Fig. I.—III. a vysv. na přední
str. příl.

Čís. II. Pletený šál. (K tomu čís. 20.)

Čís. 10. Spodní sukně z pruhované
hedvábné látky s krajkovou okrasou.
Střihový přehled Fig. IV. a V. a vysv.
na přední str. příl.

Bazar 1893, p. 82.

Nové Mody 1893, p. 1.

Czerny-ho Tanningena jest nejlepší, olova prosté, zaručené, neškodné a hned působící **barvivo na vlasy** vousy, jakož i brvy, jež nejprostším způsobem, pouze po jediném upotřebení určité a jisté obdrží zase tutéž bezvadnou, lesklou, rusou, hnědou nebo černou barvu přirozenou, jižto měly před sešedivěním a jež nepozbití ani při mytí mýdlem, ani v parní lázni, po zl. 2.50 kr., líčidla na pleť, pudry, krémy, voňavky atd. ⸺ Zákonné chráněno ⸺ Vyrábí se výhradně a jest pravé k dostání u Ant. J. Czerny-ho, Vídeň, město, Wallfischgasse 5.
Zásylky bezodkladné na dobírku, prospekty dle přání zdarma a franko. — Zakázky od 5 zl. počínaje franko. — Sklady v lékárnách v Praze: u Fürsta na Poříčí, u Koberta na Můstku, u Fragnera v Ostruhové ul., Trutnov: Czerný, v Jablonci n. N.: Satrapa, Tanzer. Olomouc: Schroetter, Brno: Wlasák, Grolich, Jihlava: Inderka, Budějovice: Wallesky, Písek: Janouš, Opava: Ponec, Pohl. (Pravé jen s jmenem Antonín J. Czerny.)

čís. 5. Pláštěnka se sametovými límci do plesu.

mnohé ještě překvapení, které bude naše abonentky těšiti. Neváhejme ještě o dalších plesových nádherách se umluviti. Rukavice, které dosahují ku krátkým vydutým rukávkům, jsou z bílé kůže; světlé, barevné řídí se dle barvy celé toilety. Hořejší jich okraj zdoben jest krajkami, zlatými nitmi, úzkými stuhami aneb vyšíváním. Často vidíme zlatem vyšité kytice, z nichž jedna jest na okraji rukavice, druhá kytice blíže prstů vyšita. Hedvábnými krajkami, jakož i stuhami jsou také ruka vice zdobeny. Tkané rukavice jsou vyšity hedvábím, aneb prolamované (à-jour) hedvábím. Nejoblíbenější barva tohoto druhu jest vanilkově žlutá. Kytice do vlasů i na prsa jsou z bílých květů voleny. — Zvláštní obliby docházejí mechové růže, fialky a karafiáty, buďto každý druh zvlášť, anebo tyto tři druhy pospolu v kytici upravené. Rozumí se, že míníme kytice z čerstvých květin. Kdo dá přednost květinám umělým, volí pomněnky, eriky, růže, které jsou stuhami propleteny a různým způsobem za okrasu upraveny. Jmenované tyto květiny jsou v kytice svázány, často malými, zlatými, aneb třpytnými křidélky zdobeny. Střevíčky i punčochy přizpůsobí se dle barvy toilety. Střevíce zhotovují se z téže látky co šaty, nejsou-li tyto z příliš tenké látky. Punčochy nosí se vyšité malými, něžnými kvítky, aneb prolamované (à-jour). Ze šperků nejvíce oblíbeny jsou perlové náhrdelníky, aneb na zcela tenkém zlatém řetízku jsou upraveny perle a tyrkysy v různých kombinacích. Nejnovější, avšak dosud málo napodobená moda jest, že nosí dámy na nohou nad kotníky navlečené spony na způsob stříbrných hadů. Vějíře pro mladé dívky jsou nejvíce gázové, různým způsobem stuhami zdobené; častěji jsou jen ze stuh zhotovené. Pro větší toilety jsou vějíře z pštrosích per určeny. Tyto vyjímají se prapodivně, poněvač pštrosí pera jsou zcela hladká, nikoli načechraná. První pohled na takový vějíř dělá dojem, jakoby pera byla jedním směrem kartáčována. Konečně budiž ještě zmíněno o velice praktickém plesovém předmětu. Jsou to plesové přezuvky z plsti, plyšem z úzka lemované a sponami k zapínání opatřené. Tato zpomínka jest určena pečlivým matinkám, které své miláčky před nastuzením uchraniti chtějí. Takováto přezuvka do plesu vyjímá se neméně graciosně.

Renée Francis.

čís. 6. Toiletta se širokými výložky. (Střihu k životu lze užíti označ. čís. 1. za přední straně střihové přílohy v příštím sešitě. Střihu k sukni lze užíti označ. čís. 2. na přední straně střihové přílohy k seš. 9. roč. IV.)

Bazar 1890, p. 156.

While in 1890 they were folded but tight fitting and extending the shoulder seam, in the following years they widened and became flatter at the top. In 1893 the bulge of the sleeve reached from the shoulder to the elbow and the sleeve was tight at the lower part. In 1895 the bulge was at its widest and reached furthest under the elbow. As early as in 1896 the "tie-shaped", "vase-shaped," and "pleated" type of sleeves was popular. With these sleeves the decorative widening was less apparent and moved lower towards the shoulder again.

These sleeves were decorated in various ways. The following year the sleeves were formed merely with small baloons and toward the end of the century they became completely smooth. The length of jackets and bodices varied during the 1890's. At the beginning of the period the jacket reached deep under the hips. However, in the following years jackets with very short bell-shaped tails as well as the "directoire" jackets, reaching to mid-thighs. were appreciated.

The outer garment was also subject to the fashion changes. The half-long pelerines and short paletots became more popular than long mantles. They had high collars called "Medici" and were usually of a historicizing cut. After 1895, under the influence of the Exhibition of Ethnography in Prague, the upper dress was decorated with braid embroidery in a national style and was buttoned with fastening with loops.

The garments preserved in the collection of the Museum of Decorative Arts from the period between 1889 and 1900 present a mosaic of cuts although they do not show the changes in fashion in all their variety and richness. At the very beginning we can see a recently-obtained dress inv. no. 96.784 in brown-grey satin and velvet of the princess cut of the front pieces, arranged asymmetrically toward the right hand side, where an arranged drapery hangs, decorated with a fringe. The front piece of the skirt creates bowl-shaped folds, the hips are decorated with stripes of velvet . The back piece is cut at the waist and between the tips of the back piece of the bodice a richly-folded segment of the skirt is inserted, extended into a small train. The sleeves are pleated at the top, and a bustle is sewn into the skirt. The dress belonged to the wife of a merchant from Wenceslas Square in Prague and was created around 1889. A very tight silhouette with tight-fitting bodice and broadened sleeves extending the shoulder seam

Čis. 20 Saty k vycházkám ze sevintu

Pařížské Mody
1894, no. 1.

are typical for the dress inv. no. 82.354 of wine-red taffeta and cream-white woollen lace from around 1890. The skirt is made of vertical stripes of taffeta and lace, and on the reverse side strings for suspending are sewn on. One very interesting example is an olive-green dress in corded silk inv. no. 69.380. It is a two-piece dress with a rich shawl flounce of black lace and green guipure with tubular extending sleeves reaching to the elbow and a slightly extended skirt. It was created in Marie Kovaříková's workshop in Hořice around 1892. Another similar one is the grey and white woollen striped dress inv. no. 50.892 with shawl flounce covering the shoulders, the sleeves pleated toward the elbow and a moderately bell-shaped skirt decorated with flounces. It very much resembles the dresses from fashion magazines designed for sports. Approximately between 1892 and 1893 the wedding dress of Empire style inv. no. 49.945 was created with an arranged bow of wide sash at the breast, resembling an illustration in the "Bazar" magazine no. 18, 1892, illustration no. 17, marked "according to the taste of Marie Louise". The girl's evening dress of cream-white damask inv. no. 97.303 has large oval neckline with flounce hemline and with short, richly-pleated sleeves. The dress is of princess cut with a number of overeasts at the waist. It was created at Mrs. M. Štěpánková's workshop in Chrudim probably around 1894. It is surprising that in our collection there are not any dresses typical of the period between 1895 and 1896 with wide shoulders and an extraordinarily broadened skirt. It is possible that such a dress would have been too demanding and showy affair within the modest

Číslo 7. — V Praze, dne 29. března 1895.

Modní převěsky a nová stinítka.

Co si máme voliti z toho víru krásných, stále nových tvarů? Vskutku těžko jest nám rozhodnouti, nebo vítězství, jež nyní slaví velitelka moda svým vybraným vkusem a svou vzletnou fantasií, jeví se v jarních modách opět na novo. Veliký obraz ve středu tohoto čísla Bazaru jest věrným zrcadlem jarních mod, obsahuje bohatý výběr elegantních převěsků, obleků a veškerých, pro dokonalou jarní toiletu potřebných předmětů. Ačkoliv se nám zdá, že se moda poněkud mírní vzhledem k pestrosti a živosti barev, musíme se tím více obdivovati rozmanitosti a rychlému střídání nových modních střihů a moderním okrasám, jež se vyskytují již tak záhy z jara, že se dá tušiti napřed, jakou hojnost novotin nám opět přinese toto období. Nejprvnější dary štědré paní mody skládají se z příslušných, pro počasí vhodných převěsků, paletek a lehčích plášťů, jež se hodí i později k teplejším dnům. Paletka, která se nosí skoro vesměs krátká a jednoduchá, jsou určena hlavně pro mladší dámy, kdežto starší dámy dávají přednosť delším pelerynám, pláštěnkám a képům.

Nechceme t. dámy, naopak, ného provedení mladistvé ztepil všech barvách; z perforovaného šívkou, u níž Nejoblíbenější modrá s červeno s červenou, písl revnou a jiné po

Tyto límce nebo se vyšívají zlaté šňůry a jir zvláštní novinku revným podklad se opatří obnov tyto jsou ronber pínají se třpytný nými vázankami mítu, hedvábné ozdobeny bohaté hedvábného gáz věradla bohatých vených růží, kop

Velice pěkn je opatřena vyz vého hedvábí od široké vložky z zapíná se též p růží. Hrdelní v ryšky a perlami. vyšívání a pliso máče ze splývaj v bohaté náhrdel — ano, zdá se, ladných peleryn Vesně.

Délka těcht od krátkých jen k oněm peleryn derní paletka m jsou pouze v zač též přiléhající p již tak přehnané u kabátů mužsky límci v podobě šá Jiná paletka ma Veškerá moderní zhotovují se z satynu, reversibl

Paladrány, a žaketům. Nej volných paletek pláště, jež jsou s lejší části. Tyto drány zhotovují s době paletka a r opatří často kápí

Velmi mode: úbory tyto sklád letko těchto oble se nosí s halenk dobné úbory vyz k těmto oblekům se kolmé švy usne těchto úborů nos které se však so

K doplnění j jichž je velmi za ného svitu. Stiní stále velmi jedn vkusným provede dosud žádné vali tak jako za čast stinítek mívají m moderních stiníti z bronzu, smaltu

Praktická st příslušné k toilet hované šínírovan barevná stinítka vaných látek s b

V dnešním č stinítka. O elega čárů, na př. k ja sportovním našicí

Čís. 1. Peleryna z plisovaného a perforovaného sukna.
Vysv. na přední str. příl.

Čís. 2. Jarní úbor s krátkým paletkem.
(K tomu čís. 8.) Střih a vysv. na přední str. příl. Čís. III.
Fig. 30—35.

Čís. 3. Háčkovaný límec pro děti. (K tomu čís. 12.)

Čís. 8. Pohled ze zadu na paletko čís. 2.

Čís. 9. Vyšívaný košíček na utěrák.
Vzorový nákres na zadní str. příl. Čís. XII.
Fig. 85.

Czech surroundings. However, on the other hand, there are a number of dresses from the period between 1897 and 1899. Two dresses of plum blue taffeta (inv. no. 95.702) with black lace plastron and black velvet ribbons, and inv. no. 61.775 of grey taffeta, green plastron and white ribbons are of a similar cut. They are cut in two pieces with a short jacket decorated with a flounce shawl collar, the sleeves moderately extended at the top and a bell skirt. Both dresses probably come from Prague from between 1897 and 1898. The extraordinary popularity of dresses with the bolero cut bodice is illustrated by the dress inv. no. 61.762 from Anna Vacková workshop in Teplice, which is made of silk with a tiny pink and green pattern.

The dress of blue-grey woollen cloth with delicate sheen pattern (inv. no. 88.628), decorated with white floral design embroidery, with baloon sleeves and bell skirt, is interesting not only because of the cut, but namely because of the type of embroidery which was specified as "Slavonic". It became widespread after 1895 in connection with the Exhibition of Ethnography in Prague. It was created at Mrs Ludmila Hospodářová workshop, founded in 1879 in Ferdinand avenue in Prague. This workshop was awarded a golden medal at the Anniversary Regional Exhibition in 1891.

Unfortunately there is not any suit or tailored cloth dress from this period preserved in our collection, but we do have a lot of jackets, mantles and capes, made mostly of black silk materials and lace.

Bazar 1895, p. 148.

Čís. 21. Peleryna s ohrdlíkem z kožešiny, pak čís. 22, biryt pro mladé dámy.
Stihový přehled Fig. I. a vysv. na přední str. příl.

Čís. 23. Oblek s krátkým paletkem, určený k vycházkám, pak čís. 24, plstěný klobouk.
Střih a vysv. na zadní str. příl. Čís. IX. Fig. 49—57.

Čís. 25. Dlouhé paletko s kožešinovými lemovkami, pak čís. 26, plstěný klobouk toque.
Střih a vysv. na přední str. příl. Čís. II. Fig. 16—21.

Čís. 27. Šaty ze sukna a karbovaného aksamítu, pak čís. 28, plstěný klobouk s pérovou okrasou.
Vysv. na zadní str. příl.

Čís. 29. Paletko se slovanským šňůrkováním, pak čís. 30, plstěný klobouk pro mladé dámy.
(K tomu čís. 54.) Vysv. na zadní str. příl.

Čís. 31. Peleryna s námětkovým vyšíváním a kožešinovou okrasou, pak čís. 32, kápě pro starší dámy.
Střih a vysv. na zadní str. příl. Čís. XV. Fig. 92—95.

Dress of wine-red
taffeta
and woolen lace.
Bohemia around 1890,
inv. no. 82.354.

Bolero dress.
Anna Watzek workshop,
Teplice around 1897,
inv. no. 61.762.

Grey-white striped dress.
Moravia 1892,
inv. no. 50.892.

Novotiny ✶ ✶ ✶
❀ hotových oděvů pro dámy
k podzimnímu a zimnímu období
v bohatém výběru a nejlevnějších cenách
doporoučí
velectěným damám
velkozávod s damskou konfekcí
Julius Zikan
v Praze,
v Celetné ul. čís. 19,
vedle kavárny „U červeného orla".

FASHION BETWEEN 1900 and 1906

Women's fashion entered the new century with a slim silhouette, emphasizing the form of a woman's body. "We notice with pleasure that this year it seems that many new fashion clothes have a certain graceful character of tasteful simplicity and modest appearance which cultivates women's beauty and proves it sometimes more effectively than the abundance of decorations and the search of bizarre compositions of clothes," writes the fashion reporter of "Bazar" on 29 December 1899. The still popular blouse bodices, loose boleros and waistcoats with a little hitch-up in the front and at the waist and also plain skirts extended to make a train, with generous pleats at the waist of the back piece created the typical art nouveau gooseneck line of the woman's figure in the first few years of the 20th century. The World Exhibition in Paris in 1900 became an extraordinary event in the development of fashion as it provided a retrospective view of the past as well as a survey of the most modern fashion trends. All the Prague magazines gave detailed information about the event and fashion magazines published reviews and numerous illustrations of exhibited models from most famous Parisienne workshops, such as Worth, Doucet, Paquin, Felix and others. Great interest was shown in the Palais de Costume, where the history of clothing was demonstrated on newly-made costumes from clothes woven after the old patterns in Lyon. The development of fashion lines between 1902 and 1906 brought a gradual loosening of

Nové
Pařížské
Mody
1905.

Obr. 61.—63 Spodní sukně z

the slim, compact silhouette of the first few years of the 20th century. "Fashion proceeds in widened shapes slowly, but continually, and as we can see our ladies are slowly getting used to this change. What seemed to be impossible to them a year ago, is now recognized as inevitable and nice..."[81/]

The bodice widened and was more gathered and hitched into the shape of goose breast, with a high pleated or gathered belts and lowered shoulders. Tight-fitting sleeves, common at the beginning of the 20th century, started to widen upwards - first with a little folds at the cuffs, later with the upper part down to the elbow tight and decorated with frills, which were let out below the elbow. Around 1905 the sleeves were generously folded at the top and tight-fitting at the bottom, often gathered in both inward and outward seams in order to let the sleeve flow down in oblique folds. The skirt also followed the contemporary fashion trend. Over the years bell-shaped cuts, multi-piece cuts with flounces, radially folded cuts with folds sewn together on the upper part of the skirt and other cuts, which widened towards the bottom of the skirt, became widespread. The richness of the cut was complemented with the decorative character of the materials, amongst which the most favoured was a relief lace. Crochet lace (so-called Irish lace) became very popular as it was an affordable imitation of expensive needle lace. Irish lace was in good keeping with art nouveau aesthetics for its plastic character and patterns, which were inspired by motifs from nature. It was used on small accessories such as collars and cuffs as well as on larger pieces of dress such as blouses, bolero-jackets, cloaks, coats and summer outfits. In 1907, "Zádruha" - an association for the

Nové
Pařížské
Mody
1906.

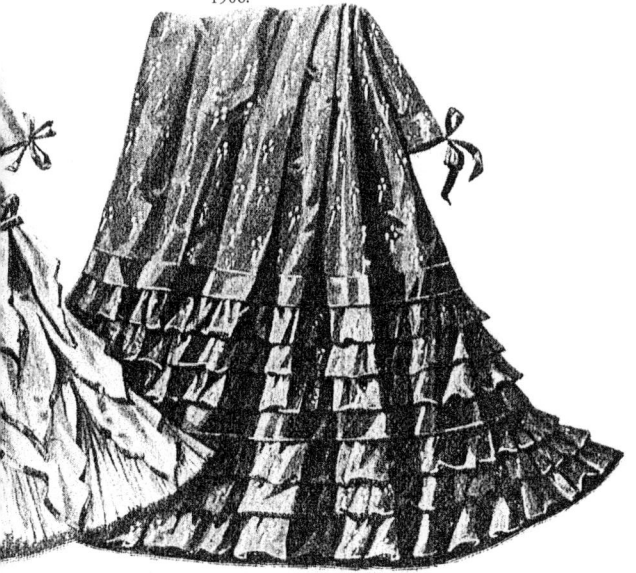

a hladké hedvábné látky.

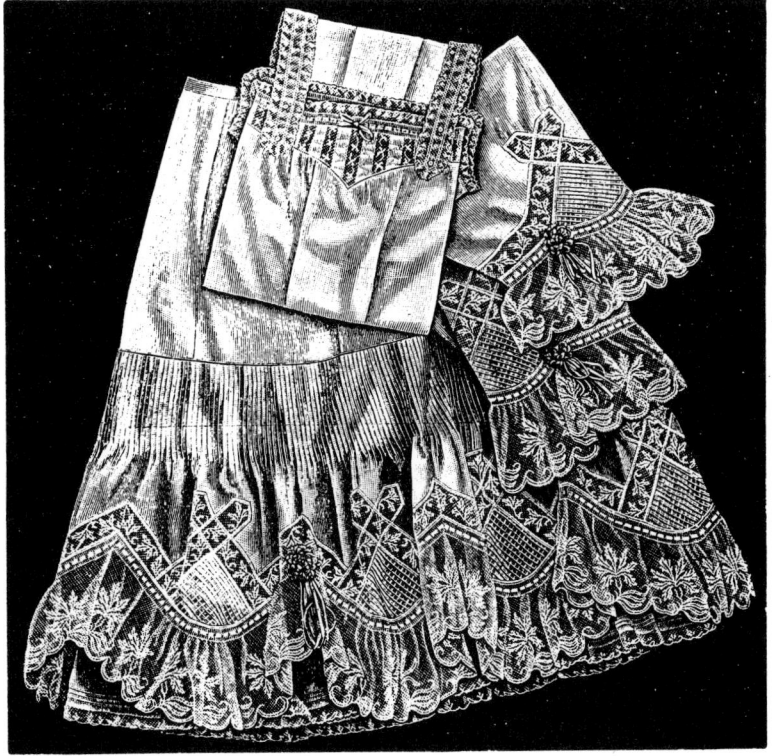

Modní síň s dámskými klobouky
otevřela v Krakovské ulici č. 25 a prosí o vzácnou přízeň ct. dam
JOSEFINA NOVÁKOVÁ,
býv. direktris fy. St. Bartoš.

support of industry influenced by folk art, called a competition for works made from Irish lace. The best pieces from the competition were displayed at the Anniversary Exhibition of the Chamber of Trade and Commerce in Prague in 1908.

At the same time as the dress, cut at the waist with the bolero or hitched up bodice, at the beginning of the century a dress in the Empire style came into fashion, classified as a "new shape dress", or "new cut dress". The dresses were recommended, at least at the beginning of the century, only to tall slim ladies, because "only on such ladies does the new cut look elegant and is legitimate."[82/] The basic cut of the short bodice and draped skirt was complemented by fashion details such as the shape of the sleeves or the richness of the skirt. At the same time as the Empire dress the "reform" dress, which was typicaly looser, also appeared.

Nové Pařížské Mody 1900, no. 23, p. 6.

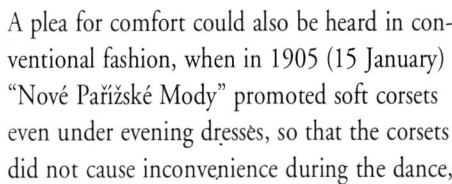

Back page.

A plea for comfort could also be heard in conventional fashion, when in 1905 (15 January) "Nové Pařížské Mody" promoted soft corsets even under evening dresses, so that the corsets did not cause inconvenience during the dance,

"Toilette of foulard with bolero...".
Nové Pařížské Mody 1900,
no. 15, p. 8. Front page.

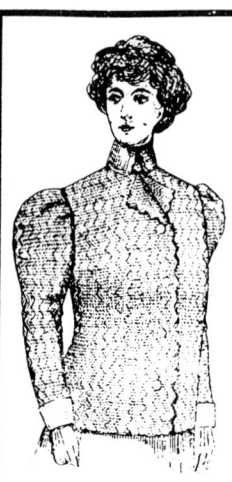

Moderní pletené žakety

čistě vlněné, v barvě krém (bílé), černé, tmavomodré a šedé, velice elegantní střih, dle velikostí kor. 15·60, 16·60, 17·60,

moderní pletené bluzy

v těchže barvách dle velikosti K 11·60, 12·80, 14·— vyrábí mechanická pletárna

JAN GLOTZ a SPOL.
PRAHA, Václavské náměstí č. 28./973.

Potřebná míra: objem pasu a prsou. :: Na venek zásilky dobírkou, nehodící se ochotně vymění. Obrázkový ceník pánských kazajek, vest, sukní, přehozů, specialit proti revmatismu, Jägrova prádla a **veškerého** pleteného i trikotového zboží zdarma a franko.

Největší sklad toho druhu v Praze.

Jan Kluge a spol.,
c. k. priv. továrna na čokoládu a cukrovinky
Praha-Smíchov.

SKLADY: PRAHA, Jungmannovo nám. 22 a Příkopy 6—8.
VÍDEŇ, Wollzeile číslo 6—8.

Doporoučí ct. pp. obchodníkům v nejlepším druhu **máčecí a kakaové hmoty,** kakaový prášek zaručeně čistý, kakaové máslo, crémové čokolády, desertní čokolády, jemné bonbony, hedvábné bonbony a všeho druhu dragée v cenách levných. — Ceník zdarma.

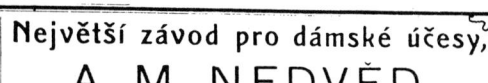

Největší závod pro dámské účesy,

A. M. NEDVĚD,
PRAHA, Nekazanka.
(Palác zemské banky.)

Shampoonování (antisept. mytí hlavy s elektr. vysušováním.) Petrolování, ondulace, manicure, pedicure.

Pěstění a barvení vlasů.

= Rationelní pěstění pleti pomocí vibrační masáže. =

Umělecké vlásenkářství.

Specialita: Přední účesy a transformace. Vložky „Maria Stuart", „Heureka" a pod.

Účesové ozdoby. — Parfumerie américaine.

Telefon 3209.

Stálá výstava - - - - - -
- - - - - orig. Pařížských
bohatě zdobených modellů
a anglických klobouků sportovních
v ohromném výběru

ST. BARTOŠ,
továrna na slaměné a plstěné klobouky

PRAHA II., Příkopy č. 6 (dům pana Urbacha, mezipatro).

Prodej veškerých příprav na dámské klobouky
a formy na klobouky za tovární ceny.

Opravy se rychle vyřizují.   Opravy se rychle vyřizují.

Sklad nábytku. Založ. r. 1872 **Jan Pelíšek**
Výbavy pro nevěsty, zařizování bytů, obchodn. místností nást. František Řezníček, přísežný znalec c. k. okres. soudu v Karlíně.
a kanceláří levně a nejvkusněji provádí osvědčená firma KARLÍN, Vinohradská tř. č. 143.

Formal toilettes.
Nové Pařížské
Mody 1902, p. 111.
Front side.

but supported the body in the way demanded by the "reform fashion".

Contemporary with the draped, richly decorated dresses, English tailored suit-type garments still remained fashionable, so that "each lady could choose her dress according to her figure and taste".[83/]

Č. 52—55. Agrafy z jetu a oceli.

Formal toilettes.
Back side.

Wedding dress,
cut in the Empire style.
Nové Pařížské Mody
1905, no. 22, p. 5.

Bazar 1907, p. 137. >

However, this type of garment also changed according to fashion. The tight, classical jackets and skirts of the first decade of the century changed into looser skirts of a semi-tight-fitting cut, with the sleeves extended toward the shoulder and with pleated skirts extending in width.

Also the cuts of mantles were subject to fashion changes throughout the period. At the beginning of the century they were long, of a semi-tight-fitting cut, with narrow sleeves and a little widened toward the bottom edge. They could be complemented by pelerine collars or boleros. As the silhouette became wider, the size of the mantles changed too, especially with the evening "sortie du theater", which were similar in their cut to the wide capes of the 19th century. Throughout the Art Nouveau period in Bohemia mantles were popular made of homespun, tweed or cloth, which continued the tradition of the very popular pelerines of the 1890's. They represented a multipurpose kind of informal dress, used by women of all social groups.

na levém háčkovou závěrkou. Ohraničeny 1 cm šir. šikmo střiženým pruhem uzavírají náprsník napřed i vzadu špičatý a zdobený stojatými záložkami ve skupinách. Jemné écru špachtlové vložky a sezáhybovaný zelený pruh hedvábný zdobí stojatý límec opatřený kolmými záložkami.

Rukávy z vrchní látky ve dvojité výdutky upravené nabrány jsou v hlavičky, jež upevněny jsou k rukávům spodním. Na levém dolním předním okraji halenky hladkým dílem ukryta jest malá kapsička na hodinky.

Čís. 14 a 12. Anglický paletový kostým.

Pro velikost 48 třeba asi 8 m látky 130 cm šir., 17 m prýmků 2 cm šir. a 20 cm šikmo stříženého černého sametu.

Čís. 9. Kratší kostým se sametovou vestou a odlišným reverovým límcem.
(Pohled ze zadu vyobr. 9a.)

Čís. 10. Podzimní paleto tvaru poloempirového.
(Pohled ze zadu vyobr. 10a.)

K úpravnému paletu se světlou hedvábnou podšívkou voleno jest sukno střední barvy. Přední a zadní díly zaštepovány jsou částečně v stejné záhyby (viz pohled ze zadu). Pás 3½ cm široký vzadu obloukovitě se stýkající kryje nášev šosu, který opatřen jest vzadu záhyby. Tento vyznačuje se s předními okrajovými pruhy souhlasným štepováním. Bílé soukenné pruhy 1 cm široké ohraničují soukennou vestu, která v ozdobném vzoru krášlena jest tmavším sutaškovým nebo hedvábným vyšíváním. Zoubcový límec a náručky polodlouhých rukávů vypouklých zhotoveny jsou z tmavé kůže (nebo napodobeniny kožené) a na okrajích 1½ cm široko zdobeny bílým suknem, jakož i s tímto současně vedenou bílou sutaškou. Závěrku vesty tvoří fantasijní knoflíky.

Čís. 11 a 13. Jupičkový kostým s halenkou.

Na kostým velikosti 43 třeba asi 5¾ m látky 120 cm šir., 40 cm sametu šikmo stříženého, 4¾ m podšívkového hedvábí 50 cm šir. a 6 knoflíků; na halenku asi 5 m hedvábí 50 cm šir. a 40 cm krajky 4 cm šir.

Halenka ze zeleného, jemně květovaného čínského hedvábí vzoru pruhovaného doplňuje praktický kratší kostým ze šedozelené kostkované anglické látky vlněné. Jupička tvaru polopřiléhavého pracována jest s anglickým ševním dělením. Střední díly jsou k pobočním naštepovány. Dle obrysů jejich tvořice úzký Kellerův šev připojeny jsou okrasné díly bez podšívky, které vpředu a vzadu se zúžují k dolejšku a sahají až k několikráte proštepovanému okraji jupičky. Malý šálový límec a náručky rukávů kyjovitých přiměřeně široko-

Čís. 9a.

Čís. 12. Živůtek ke kostýmu vyobr. 14.

Čís. 13. Halenka k vyobr. 11.

Čís. 10a.

Čís. 14. Anglický paletový kostým s jednoduchým šosovým živůtkem a prýmkovou okrasou. (K tomu vyobr. 12.)

FASHION BETWEEN 1907 and 1914

The wave of orientalism, which began to spread from France around 1905 into all areas of art, and was supported by the influence of the Djagilev's Russian ballet which enchanted Paris in 1909, also influenced fashion. Another aesthetic stream of the neoclassicist period also provided inspiration for Paris fashion designers, the most renowned of whom was Mr Paul Poiret. The French style "directoire" and Greek draped arrays[84] were the specific inspiration sources. Out of a combination of these styles, similar by the fact that they all respected the demands of the reform tendencies, a new silhouette of women's dress developed (this had happened in Paris around 1907), which then lasted for several years.

The new cut was composed of a short bodice, put together with loose, intricate pieces, folded up over each other in front, with comfortable kimono sleeves cut from one piece with the front and back pieces and a long skirt of princess cut fitting the woman's figure tightly high upon the waist. The skirt was straight, with a tunic or an overskirt, and with a train if it was an evening dress. The informal, relaxed and graceful look of the new silhouette was achieved by the overlapping of light materials such as silk, lace and tulle, and by decorations of silk braids, lace guipurs or machine embroidery. In 1907 the fashion reporter Yvonna wrote with appraisal in "Národní Politika" that "Finally the competent hands of artists have taken over the leadership in fashion",[85] but "Nové Pařížské Mody" did not accept the change with the same enthusiasm. The reporter criticised the simplicity of the new fashion with the remark that the dress, composed of individual pieces of cloth tightly fitting the figure, gave the impression that the woman's figure was enfolded in the cloth. He also considered the height of the collars tasteless, which,

Nové Pařížské Mody 1910 - 1911.

České Mody 1914, p. 12.

34 35 36 37

i jiným; kdo nepěstuje pořádek, rozzlobí sebe a jiné, stává se nepříjemným člověkem, kterého se každý rád zbaví. Kariéra mnohých, štěstí životní, bylo zničeno nepořádkem. Sirky, dávané na určité místo, ukazují hned celého člověka, vědomého svého i nejnepatrnějšího činu a tudíž spolehlivého; člověk, jenž pohodí ledabyle krabičku sirek, aniž by dbal do druhého dne státi. Jsou-li slupky neporušeny a jablka před vařením řádně otřena, možno je spolu vařiti. Příštího dne procedí se kaše žíněným sítem a na každý 1 tr šťavy přidá se půl kg cukru. Směs se vaří tak dlouho, až kapka, byvši na porculán spuštěna, brzy ztuhne. Za horka plní se do láhví.

TANGO-CORSET

(normální linie)

předčí svou vynikající elegancí a dobře přiléhající formou všechny ostatní šněrovačky a proto mu náleží přednost. — Tango-šněrovačka jest téměř ve všech lepších příslušných obchodech k dostání.

Továrna na šněrovačky

Federer & Piesen

Praha VII.

Sklady. Ovocná ul. 19. Celetná ul. 17.

Vývoz do všech dílů světa!

Bujná ňadra

ve dvou měsících použitím „**Pilules Orientales**'

(pilulek východních), jediných které napomáhají vývoji, tuhosti a obnově poprsí a propůjčují i prsům vdaných dam graciosní plnosti, beze všeho ohrožování zdraví. Zaručeně bez přímesku otrušíku. Nejvěhlasnějšími lékaři uznány. Naprostá diskretnost. Krabička s návodem K 6·45 franko. **J. Ratié**, lékárník v Paříži. Sklady: **Budapešť, J. V. Török,** 12 Kiraly utza; **Vídeň, R. Pserhofer,** Singerstrasse 15.

Český Svět 1914.

Nové Pařížské
Mody 1905,
no. 22, p. 9.

according to his opinion, exceeded all limits, because it sometimes reached up over the chin and thus covered the lower part of the face... He considered the hat to be another offence to good taste, as it was worn low over the forehead and had nearly the same diameter as the skirt. He was worried that the plump bodies of Czech beauties would be too susceptible to the critics, and that this cut would not cover the imperfections of figure of slim ladies either, because "this cut does not hide the shape of the body, but, on the contrary, reveals it". He came to the conclusion that such a fashion was not elegant and should be condemned.

However, at the beginning of his article he admitted that new fashion always makes an unpleasant impression and that the ladies have to get used to the novelties and slowly and gradually appraise their virtues.[86/]

The new silhouette did not become popular easily in Bohemia, but slowly it became accepted in 1907 by the gradually rising waist and the acceptance of kimono sleeves. "The victory of the Japanese style has also reached fashion. The typical sign of the Japanese style - kimono sleeves - appear on all robes",[87/] wrote Jan Kratina in "Damské Modní Listy". Some characteristic features from the period before still appeared - the skirt was still very rich and the kimono sleeve was combined with wide sleeves, inserted under the shoulder. In 1908 Jan Kratina reported that the Japanese influence had withdrawn, but the kimono remained popular, complemented by byzantine tunics. He also noticed the glittering colours of the

Nové Pařížské
Mody 1907,
no. 22, p. 7.

u šeříkovým
em. Výstřih vytuje sedlo z bío tylu. Úzký
nteclerový lí
ček z pravých
jek souhlasí
nanšetami ru
/ů, které jsou
iženy v celku
životem. Pás
zhotoven ze
hy; sukně je
norní části uita v záložky
oo straně dole
mo zastřižena,
že je vidět
odní dolní díl
kně. Široká
nda přidržuje
ιyby sukně
d koleny. Klo
ιk slaměný je
spodní straně
echy potažen
íkovým same
ι a jedinou
lobou jeho je
natá rajka.
Druhý oblek
z černého kraj
/ého tylu a tmavozeleného atlasu liberty. Pás a po
ιnní ovruba vrchní krajkové tuniky jsou zhotoveny
erného sametu. Sukně je sestavena ze dvou přes
ιe splývajících částí, z nichž dolní vzadu je zdrhnuta
podkasána.
né krajky zdosukni dle vyazení. Klo
ιk z černé
ιhledné slámy
ozdoben černi sametkami
/ěncem stíno
ιých růží.
Třetí toileta
jednoduchý
ek z hedváb
ιo popelínu se
:ní nahoře
ádanou a na
ním kraji krajrou vložkou
lobenou. Bluza
ozdobena satkami a vyší
ιým batisto
ι límečkem.
Čtvrtý oblek
.hotoven z pruraného světle
édého atlasu
erty a ozdoben
širokou kraj
ι chantilly téže
vy. Bluza je

je zhotoven
z chrpově modrého voálového
musselínu a černých krajek. Má
náprsníkovou
bluzu a zdrhovanou sukni v pase
i ve výši kolen.
Ozdoben je
v horní části bluzy a dole na sukni
černou krajkovou
látkou.
Poslední oblek z oloveně
šedého grenadinu
je ozdoben krajkou, přibarvenou
do téhož odstínu,
šeříkovou sametovou stuhou,
úzkými volánky
a sametovými
knoflíky.
Klobouk obr. 3.
jest černým sametem potažen a
ozdoben bílou
krajkovou vázankou a růžovou
guirlandou. Klobouk obr. 4. je černý sametový s růžemi, klobouk obr. 5.
je toque z musselínového chiffonu s bílými pštrosími
pery a poslední široký klobouk z bílého hedvábí ozdoben
je bílým musselínem a velikou růží.

**Odebírejte
a čtěte
Pestrou knihovnu
zábavy a kultury.**

Redakcí
Em. šl. z Lešehradu.

Vychází týdně.
Cena každého
svazku 20 hal.

K dostání u všech
knihkupců, zejména
u nakladatele

A. Hynka v Praze,
Celetná ul. 11.

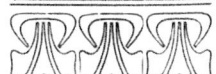

"Elegant Paris dresses".
Nové Pařížské Mody 1910,
no. 20, p. 12.

Nové Pařížské
Mody 1910,
no. 18, p. 8.

cloths and the spectacular character of golden embroidered decorations.[88/] However, the published models still had long skirts and the kimono sleeves were narrow and very long. Only in 1909 did the "directoire" style and Empire style win through at last and the silhouette narrowed and closed. Modern dames preferred stretch underwear to silk underwear because "each detail helps the beautiful outline of the human body to be emphasized".[89/] The cut did not change much in the following period. The waist still remained raised high, and only as late as in 1912 did it begin to move down again. From the beginning the camisole was very short, decorated with wide collars covering the shoulders in the way of a classicist fichu, made of tulle, silk, satin, chiffon or the same material as the dress. Around 1910 long fitted tunics appeared, fitting the body from the top under the hips. With the evening robes the fitted princess cut called robe foureau was also popular. The sleeves still had the narrow kimono cut and only in 1912 did the sleeve end under the shoulder where it was connected to a narrow, classical sleeve. The skirt, however, kept its narrow silhouette, being either only moderately pleated or divided by ironed folds or decoratively-arranged pieces decorated with rows of buttons. The change appeared between the years 1912 and 1913 when peg-top skirts draped on the hips and diminishing in width toward the ankles came into fashion. The draping was achieved by creating horizontal pleats in the front and at the back above the waist. The pleats were loose around the hips. The skirts with tunic, which was tucked up or draped, became very popular at the same time. Together with low-placed shoulders this skirt created the egg-shaped silhouette of the following years.

Damské Modní
Listy 1909,
no. 11, p. 2.

The new style also effected the suits where, together with classical cuts with narrow skirt and straight jacket, jackets appeared buttoned above the waist with round, widely open front pieces. There was also a renaissance in the combination of blouses and skirts, which complied with the basic fashionable cut of the period. The blouses were made of various materials - silk, decorated with print or embroidery, cotton batiste, or estamine, decorated with open work or white embroidery. One novelty was the elimination of standing collars - the blouses had either a small oval neckline or folded collars. Sailor-shape collars were very popular as well as large, wide and long collars on the estamine blouses. In the pre-war period and the first years of the war the so-called "svéráz" movement became active, the centre of which became the afore-mentioned cooperative "Zádruha", which aimed at the revitalization of the traditional techniques used in textile production and other kinds of folk art. Its embroidery with a styled folk ornament appeared on dresses, but even more frequently on estamine and batiste blouses of the modern cut.

The garments of the first decade of the 20th century ranks among the largest sets in the collection of the Museum of Decorative Arts in Prague. A very important part of this collec-

Damský Modní
Obzor 1913,
no. 15, pp. 20 - 21.

"New shapes of blouses from batiste, tulle, satin, liberty cloth or woolen cloth".
Nové Pařížské Mody 1910, no. 11, p. 11.

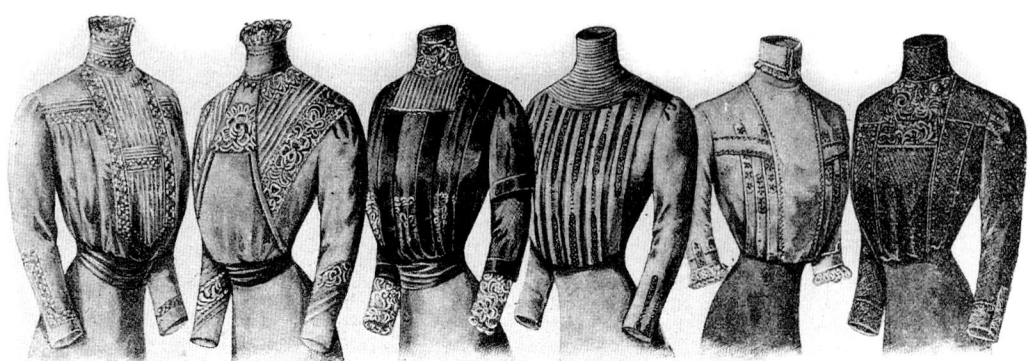

"New shapes of skirts made of English woolen material..."
Nové Pařížské Mody 1910, no. 11, p. 10.

Damský Modní
Obzor 1913,
no. 16, p. 17.

PREMIE. P. T. odběratelky a odběratelé tohoto listu obdrží právě vyšlé nádherné francouzské album „**LA MODE DE PARIS**", pro období podzimní a zimní 1913/14, obsahující 1000 různých vyobr. dámských úborů, jako: žaketů, plášťů, bluz, sukní, obleků smutečních, svatebních, plesových, dětských a j. v. za přípl. **2 K**.

112. Úbor do společnosti. **113.** Žaketový úbor s plyšovou ozdobou. **114.** Úbor zdobený prýmky. **115.** Odpolední úbor.

112 112a. Úbor do společnosti, zhotovený z pestře barevného kažmíru lososově růžové barvy a hedvábného kažmíru té samé barvy. Vpředu na živůtku skříženy jsou dva pruhy týlu. Látku živůtku stříháme v celku s rukávy, výstřih lemujeme šířeji látkou a silnou krajkou barvy slonové kosti. K živůtku přisazená sukně jest 1·70 cm široká, lehké drapování přednice kryje proužek látky, pošitý knoflíky a ohraničený dírkovanými kraji. Drapování sukně vzadu kryjí dva cípy ze vzorkovaného hedvábí, stříhané v rozměru 13/45 cm. a upravené na způsob šerpy. Sukně jest v pasu čtyřikrát zdrhnuta a výš kolem pasu 6 cm. vysoký.

113—113a. Žaketový oblek s plyšovou ozdobou, zhotovený z rypsu modré barvy. Límec, výložky rukávů a knoflíky na zadu hotovíme z plyše stříbrošedé barvy. Přední díly žaketu stříháme v celku se šosem, druhé díly přednic stranních díle a zadu jsou krátké a zadní šos stříháme též zvlášť. Zadní díl zúžen jest v pasu záševky. Žaket řízen jest až ke krku k zapínání a otevřený jest klopami. Přednice i zadek čtyřdílové sukně tvoří látkou podložené a prostehované záhyby a v horní části všita jest do pasu 6 cm. širokého a řízeného perleťovou sponou k zapínání.

114—114a. Prýmky zdobený úbor ze sukna švestkově fialové barvy. Náprsenku z týlu kryje „jabot" ze zdrhované krajky. Látka živůtku tvoří na rameni po jednom dutém záhybu a rukávy jsou do průramku hladce podloženy. Přednice ložený jsou přes sebe a levá má šálový límec potažený hedvábím, kdežto pravou zdobíme prýmky, pošitými kuličkovými knoflíky. Stejná ozdoba jest na rukávech s krajkovými náběrami a na přednici sukně, jejíž spojení se živůtkem kryje kožený pás fialové barvy se sponou. Sukně jest třídílová, v předu lehce drapovaná a zadní díl má na jedné straně záhyb.

115—115a. Odpolední úbor ze zeleného poplínu, zdobený kostkovanou látkou. Vložku vpředu tvoří knoflíky pošitý a 7 cm. širokou krajkou zdobený pruh týlu. Látku živůtku stříháme v celku, límec hotovíme z kostkované látky a přednice pošijeme ozdobnými knoflíky. Bílý proužek lemování přednic zdobí sklenené knoflíky a poutka ze šňůrek. Hedvábím lemované rukávy končí výdutkem z týlu a krajkou. Hedvábím „Gloria" podložená sukně jest vpředu drapovaná.

Kratinovy módní listy a střihy jsou, jak všeobecně uznáno, nejlepší!

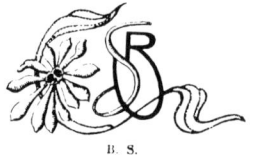

tion is represented by the models of clothes from Vienna, for example the evening and ball robes from G. A. Spitzer's fashion house, suits made by Franz Kral's Nachfolger, suits and cloaks of M. Hansalová, A. Rennerová, L. & H. Laufer and others, which reveal that demanding orders, above all from aristocratic circles, were oriented towards Viennese workshops. A much smaller representation in the collection belongs to German production, not to mention French production. The most remarkable French piece is a black georgette evening coat from the Worth workshop from 1912 - 1913 (inv. no. 70.286).

It is rather difficult to choose representative examples amongst approximately 300 dresses of Czech or most probably Czech origin. The collection includes perhaps almost all variations of cuts that appeared between 1900 and 1914.

A suit from whitish corded silk with red embroidery (inv. no. 85.973), which was made around 1900, is excellent for its typical Art Nouveau gooseneck line, although, as the application of cut embroidery motifs reveal, the suit was made from older used material. Two dresses (inv. no. 81.371), made from striped grey fabric around 1905, and a formal silk lilac dress (inv. no. 82.370), made by K. Dědic in Prague around 1908, reveal that despite a hesitating approach towards the reformistic style, this kind of dress was made and worn in Prague. Formal dress from violet silk (inv. no. 70.797), made in the workshop of B.

Wedding dress
of A. Martenová-Kopalová.
Prague 1912. Photo,
inv. no. 91.490.

Wedding dress
with bolero, grey, woolen.
Photo. Prague 1906,
inv. no. 91.078.

Dress in whitish corded silk
with red embroidery.
Bohemia around 1900,
inv. no. 85.593.

Formal dress of violet silk.
Workshop Božena Troníčková,
Prague around 1907, inv.
no. 70.797.

Reformist dress of violet corded silk.
Workshop Karel Dědic,
Prague around 1908,
inv. no. 82.370.

Grey-white striped dress,
reformist cut.
Propably Prague around 1905,
inv. no. 81.371.

Ballroom dress.
M. Doleželová workshop,
Olomouc 1912, inv. no.
86.430.

Troníčková in Prague around 1907, is one of the early examples of the use of kimono sleeves. It is interesting to follow the development of fashion lines in the wedding dress, of which there is a large number of pieces from this period still preserved. The wedding dress (inv. no. 91.484) from the workshop of M. Dvořáková is an example of a loose silhouette of 1905. The dress has a richly hitched bodice, wide puff sleeves and a bell-shaped skirt, and it was made up from a embroidered tulle and taffeta. This dress belonged to a dancer from the National Theatre.

A more modest type of dress from the same period is represented by a two-piece grey woollen wedding dress (inv. no. 91.078), made in Prague in 1906, with folded skirt and folded bolero, and complemented with a white blouse. It belonged to a bride from a middle-class Prague family.

The dress of the bride of the founder of the scout's organization from 1909 (inv. no. 91.485) already has a completely different cut - princess sheath cut. Seams are decorated with satin ornamental extension.

Another remarkable type of wedding dress is the one that belonged to the bride of the writer and critic Miloš Marten from 1912 (inv. no. 91.490). The style was influenced by the intellectual environment in which the couple lived and to which belonged such individualities as F. X. Šalda, Zdenka Braunerová, Paul Claudel and Emil Bernard, who is thought to be the designer of the dress. It has a shirt-cut and it is folded in rounded neckline and at the waist. The dress is extended into a long train which is decorated with lace. The dress is girded with wrought metal belt.

The finest example of a contemporary tailor's work is also a dress (inv. no. 86.430) made from goldish silk and metal lace. This dress was made in the workshop of M. Doleželová in Olomouc. The dress is interesting not only for its sophisticated material, but also for a peg-top cut of the skirt at the bottom, which is, nevertheless, covered with a heavy metal material of tunic. The dress was made for a dance ball in Sarajevo in 1912. A black three-piece suit from 1913 - 1914 (inv. no. 70.175) made from black corded silk and voile, decorated with ornamental embroidery, has an uncertain origin, which applies also to a summer dress with casaque bodice (inv. no. 91.084) made from creamy-white georgette and bobbin-lace. The dress dates from around 1913. Both these

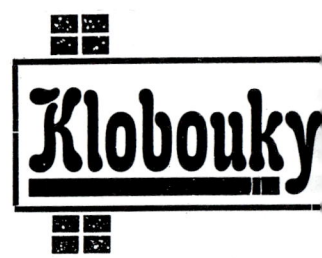

Summer complete dress, decorated with bobbin lace. Prague or Vienna around 1913, inv. no. 91.084.

Blouse of printed silk and lace. Prague or Vienna around 1913, inv. no. 91.086.

dresses were designed under the influence of Viennese fashion. A blouse from printed silk (inv. no. 91.086) comes from the same set. A blouse from Irish lace was made by Hana Jičínská in Prague between 1907 and 1908. It was made especially for the competition of the "Zádruha" association and was awarded the first prize.

A number of costume dresses in the collection reveal the popularity of fhis kind of dress in Prague and other Czech towns. The half-fitting costume (inv. no. 82.379) with widened sleeves at the top and with a bell-shaped skirt decorated with braid embroidery was made in the Prague workshop of Antonín Brtva between 1906 and 1907. The costume suit, with wide sleeves and hitched bodice sewn into a belt, was made for a mother whose child was being baptised, from Louny in 1905. The classical costume for walks (inv. no. 57.051) with a slightly widened skirt and long tight-fitting coat was made in Holešov in Moravia in the workshop of Rudolf Konečný, who was a specialist in making English costumes. The most luxurious representative of the Prague cloak production is a formal coat (inv. no. 81.370), made from greenish-grey and deep purple double cloth, which is combined with greenish-grey velvet and bobbin-lace. It was made in the Prague workshop "B. Metzeles, Hotel u černého koně, Příkopy" between 1905 and 1906.

Costume of grey loden. Louny 1905, inv. no. 92.389.

Costume. Probably workshop of Ant. Brtva, Prague around 1906, inv. no. 82.379.

J. Goth: Dance order of the ball of Czech lawyers, 3 December 1913, inv. no. GS - 16473.

Neither the clothing collection of the Museum of Decorative Arts in Prague, nor fashion production of the inter-war period significantly reflected artistic development linked with the arrival of new avantgarde artistic trends. Contemporary artistic turmoil in the field of applied arts was reflected by the foundation of the Artěl artistic association in 1908. Influenced by the Viennese association Wiener Werkstätte, Artěl's efforts were aimed at improving the artistic quality of everyday utility objects and at the revival of general public taste. Among the founding members of Artěl were textile designer M. Teinitzerová, and B. Haunerová, B. Pošepná, M. Michalcová, M. Malinová, and others joined later. Though their textile works focused primarily on interior textiles, clothing production was represented in Artěl's output of, small, batik clothing accessories and parts of clothes such as ribbons, shawls, and blouses.[90]

Formal dress of velvet.
Prague or Vienna around 1905,
inv. no. 57.701;
Evening cloak, B. Metzeles workshop,
Prague around 1905,
inv. no. 81.370.

1915 – 1918

"Problems of fashion, like many others which are not directly related to necessities of everyday life, seem to have lost their importance in the present circumstances", wrote an editor of "České Mody" magazine in his introduction to the year 1915. War obviously influenced dress in many various ways, most of them being, of course, negative, but despite this the fashion trends changed at an almost hectic pace.

One of the first signs of the war in fashion magazines was the publication of cuts of apparel for nurses and female doctors such as the apron with skirt portion buttoned at the back, and "blouse" apron or "apron" dress (working cloak). Especially in demand was a design for a uniform for field nurses which had to be practical and very warm at the same time. It consisted of a tight-fitting, double-breasted coat, buttoning closed high on the neck to keep natural body temperature in, fitted with either a hemp or leather belt, and short skirt, which a nurse could take off when it disturbed her at work, and breeches worn under the skirt. The dress was complemented with a rounded cap with peak, leather leggings with leather straps, and low waterproof shoes. The dress was made of blue cloth, the same as was used for uniforms of Austro-Hungarian army soldiers.[91/]

The war also influenced the designs for handmade works executed by women. The period before Christmas was marked by especially high interest in production of presents for field soldiers. Women knitted and crocheted headmasks, gloves with five fingers, gloves with two fingers and one large hole for shooting, and open gloves fitted with press buttons on both sides, which could have been worn either tucked up over fingers or folded. In addition, wrappers were made as well as long leggings, knee-warmers for riding, socks, socks to cover stumps of arms and legs, and home slippers. Knitted dresses were also much appreciated by female nurses in hospitals. They used knitted underwear such as bodices, sleeveless vests, underskirts, loose knitted cuffs, gloves, wrappers and shoes, and sometimes they also found use for a crocheted flask cover.

Women civilians could also help wounded soldiers with home sewing. Patterns appeared for shirts with slits placed according to the wounded body part; opening at the front for the severely wounded, shirts with cut sleeves

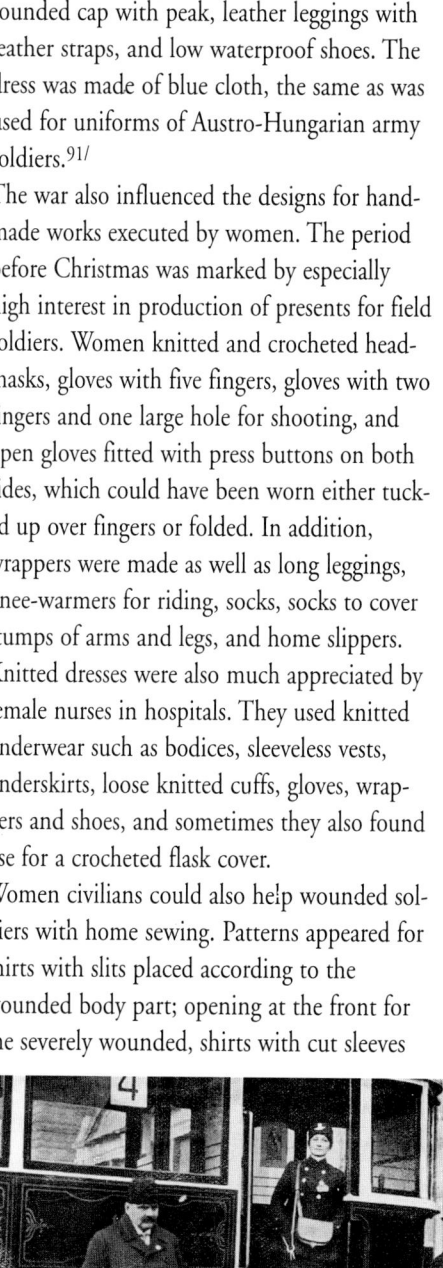

Smuteční oblek je němou prosbou raněného srdce.

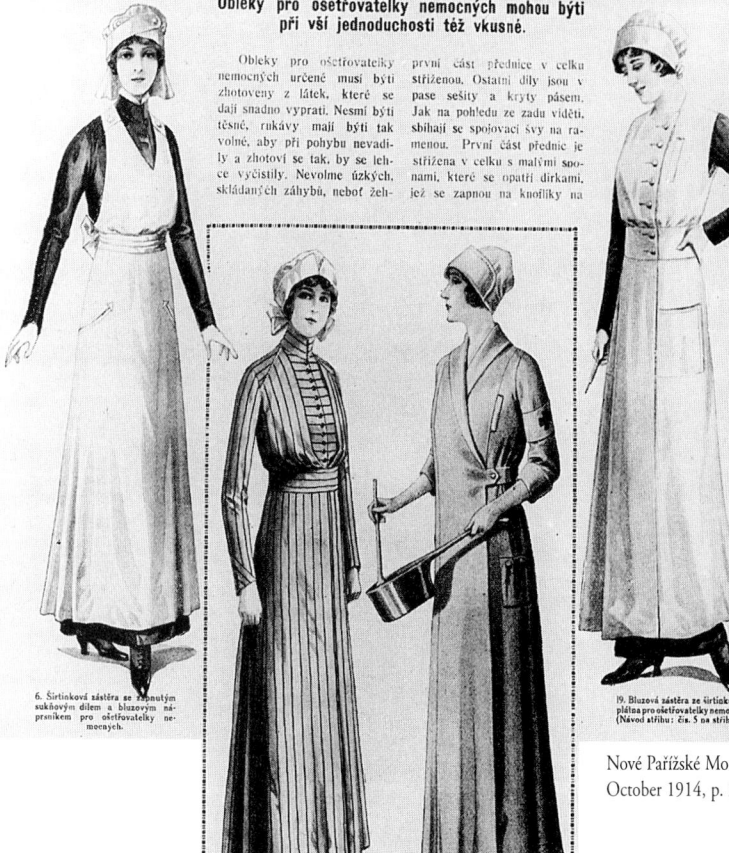

Nové Pařížské Mody, October 1914, p. 3.

Conductor on a Prague tram. Český svět, December 17, 1915.

Nové Pařížské Mody, November 1914, p. 10.

with parts connected by ribbons for soldiers with injured arms. Also, patterns for bonnets protecting the head from mosquitoes, patterns for head bandage caps, and patterns for various toiletry cases and other similar items.[92/]

As a consequence of war time, new types of dresses for various professions came to existence. Women not only took their traditional positions in hospitals, military hospitals, rehabilitation institutes for wounded soldiers, in nursing schools, baby-care centres, kitchens and public facilities providing meals, charity centres, but in many professions they had to replace men who were taken to the army. Consequently, women gradually began to work as shop assistants, shoemakers, postal workers, conductors, street-sweepers, window-cleaners, lamp-cleaners, locomotive-cleaners, etc.

In order to provide assistance to women, František Šimáček published a guide written by J. Kafka "350 ženských povolání" (350 Women's Professions) in 1916. Women's activities were carefully monitored by newspapers and magazines, such as "Český svět", which mentioned several extraordinary achievements including 13 000 plum dumplings made by ladies from Vyškov in a field hospital kitchen, or 40 cases with clothing and other presents sent to the front by the association called "Pomocný sbor města Kroměříže pro postižené válkou" (Aid Association of the City of Kroměříž for Victims of War). In 1915, the women's department of the Association of War Care in Plzeň prepared Christmas presents for 1000 soldiers in the field, women in the Red Cross in Přeštice and other local Red Cross organisations sewed underwear for field soldiers. In Pardubice, an association of housewives took care of "Vojenská domovina", an enterprise in which wounded soldiers of various nationalities gathered in order to read magazines and talk about various topics.[93/]

Although the types of dresses used at work or for voluntary humanitarian activities did not differ much from common fashion clothing, they brought many changes to the principles of modern practical apparel which were further developed. The most important features were hygiene, practicality, and comfort. That is why the selection of materials for working clothes focused on easily washed materials, patterns were simple so that the dresses could be easily maintained. One such fashion was a dress skirt or dress cloak. All types of dresses featured short, not very wide skirts, enabling free movement, they had open necks and half-length sleeves. Simple, dark dresses with white accessories, or dresses consisting of skirt and blazer or bolero and at least two changeable blouses were recommended for work in offices and shops. Corsets could not have been worn under working dress; it was recommended to use a garter belt on hips and firm lower bodice. The type of fastening also changed — little hooks, which were difficult to fasten, were replaced by buttons and somewhat simpler fastening. Women working with the ill, children, and women in kitchens were supposed to wear dresses of light colours while elsewhere dark dresses should have been worn.[94/]

Designs for mourning dresses were a sad testimony of war time. The magazine "Nové Pařížské Mody" characterised them as "silent prayer for the protection of a wounded heart".[95/] Their repeated appearance on pages of fashion magazines reflected the loss of human lives on European battlefields. They were simple walking dresses complemented with a veil and were designed according to the level of mourning. Such dresses were made either from black, or a combination of grey and black and white and black materials.

Despite the development of the war situation, which did not provide any reason for excitement, a certain level of variability

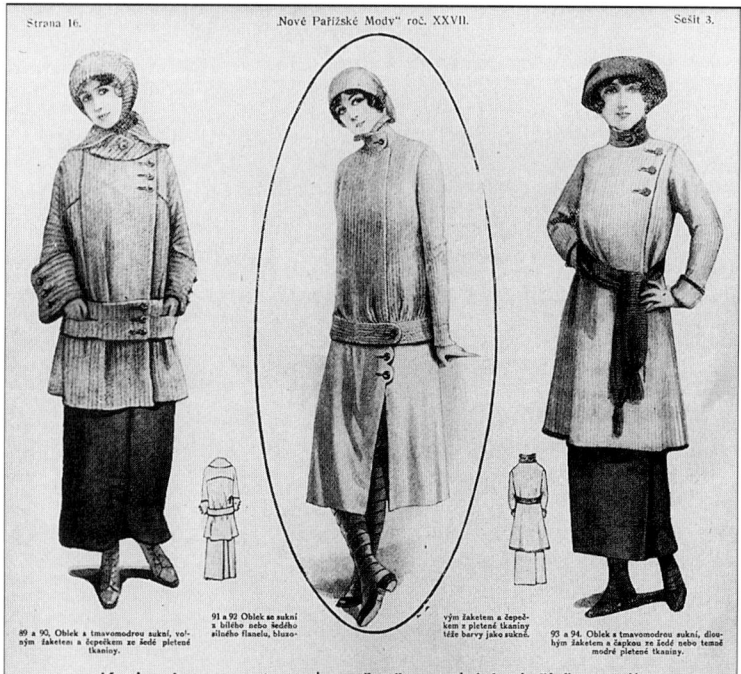

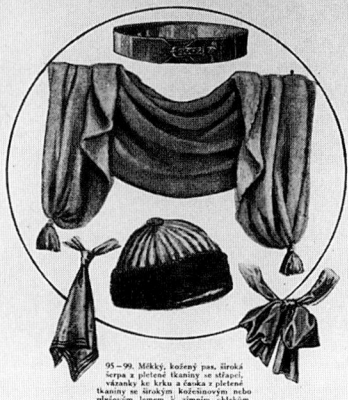

Nové Pařížské Mody, October 1915, p. 5.

Modní Svět, August 5, 1917.

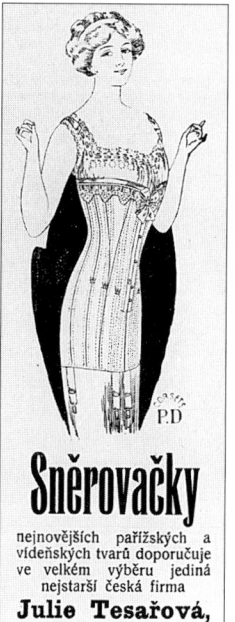

Nové Pařížské Mody, 1915—1916.

could be traced in fashion. Social events continued to take place even during the war. They included concerts, theatre performances, dance classes, and other social occasions which often had a character of charity. That is why fashion magazines devoted some attention to evening dresses for social occasions, although their attention was somewhat smaller than in peace time. Evening dresses did not differ from day dresses in their length and cut — they were rather subtle and simple. They were made from light silk materials or velvet, and the most usual colour combination was black and white. Similarly, wedding dresses also became more simple — in war time, this kind of dress could have had a form of better afternoon outfit or a costume of a fashionable cut. There were two novelties among walking dresses, one, the so-called "coat dress", and the other, a dress skirt with older blouses worn underneath. Dress consisting of a skirt and a blouse was also extremely popular. Contemporary magazines published extensive selections of sports-wear, which was certainly due to the fact that a number of kinds of sport dresses could have been used in war apparel. Warm knitted underwear, knitted jackets, waterproof jacket from tricoteen cloth padded with plush, or cap and wrapper knitted or sewn from the identical material were useful not only for a ski trip, but in any situation. Skirts, which were worn for social occasions and for a train journey, were replaced in nature by riding-type trousers complemented with rolled leggings, thick socks of pure wool, and waterproof shoes. Although designs for swimming outfits published by fashion magazines remained quite complicated, usually consisting of bodice, trunks, and little skirt, people actually used simple tricoteen swim-

České Mody, January 1915, p. 5.
Nové Pařížské Mody,
November 1914, p. 3.

ming dresses and other types of dresses which enabled the body to be exposed to the sun's rays. During the war, ideas of modern hygiene and the curing influence of water and sun became widely popular. Magazines published photographs from Czech public swimming pools and stories from various spas. The writer Karel Matěj Čapek Chod also paid certain attention to these questions when, in his novel "Jindrové", he described activities of a group of Prague artists and intellectuals, which was called "Opálka". The only aim of its members was to get their bodies as dark as possible without the use of artificial substances. The only condition of membership was not to talk about the war. Swimming costumes of its members were fully subordinate to this aim; for example ladies' swimming costumes consisted of a front and back tied with little ribbons on sides. When ladies moved, white stripes showed on their sides which contrasted with the sun-tanned parts of their bodies.[96]
Despite the proclaimed loss of the humorous character of the contemporary fashion, the development of fashion trends did not stop even during the war years. The beginning of 1915 saw all kinds of dresses complemented with skirts with various tunics which were gathered, pleated with small or large pleats, bell-shaped, serpentine, buttoned, widened at the front, with or without yoke, decorated with ribbons or embroidered edging. All types of tunics were somewhat longer, they reached at least to below knee level, but more often they went as far as the ankles. Bodices were tight-fitting, with the front parts folded over each other or fastened with buttons. They were richly decorated with small buttons. Collars were also very fashionable — they had either sharp points or were folded. The waistline was emphasised with a wide sash. Costume jackets became longer, sometimes they reached as far as the knees and they were longer at the back, while the front parts were diagonally cut. At that time, costumes were complemented with waistcoats of variously coloured materials.

Cuts of cloaks and outfits and especially details of their decoration soon became inspired by army uniforms. For example, as early as at the turn of 1914 and 1915, tight-fitting outfits with double-breasted buttoning and high folded or standing collars appeared on the fashion scene. Such outfits were decorated with braids, rows of buttons, braided fastening, decorated seams, facings, and patch breast pockets. Designs for blouses published by "České Mody" also had a military character.[97]
1915 spring fashion brought a significant change into the silhouette — wide bell-shaped skirts appeared on the scene. They were made of soft woollen materials, thin clothes, and taffe-

12. Blůzový oblek z temně modrého sukna nebo chevlotu se světle hnědým koženým pasem a odlišnými lemy. Střih k blůze a návod střihu sukně č. 7. na střihové příloze.

zapnuta vzadu, blůza pak vpředu zlatými knoflíky. Žaket obleku na vyobr. čís. 11. má našité ramenní díly, lem. odliš. proužkem. Sukně má vpředu a vzadu vprostřed šev- lemovaný. Šňůrkou a je vzadu zapnuta stiskacími knoflíky. Tento oblek je velice vkusně doplněn temnými sametovými pruhy, které se našijí na límeček a manžety

tas and they gradually shortened to calf level, and were supported by a petticoat. Bodices were tight-fitting, and had somewhat lowered shoulders and a narrow waist, which was emphasised by wide bands and sashes. Outfits were also made with bell-shaped or pleated skirts and with either half tight-fitting or loose blazers of various length. Most modern were short jackets with bell-shaped tails and "Spencer" or "bolero" blazers. Cloaks had a straight cut with or without an applied waistline, and cloaks of a loose, bell-shaped cut also appeared.

New fashion resembled the typical Biedermeier silhouette and already at that time it was considered to have a link with the war's political situation which disturbed the long and well-established dominant position of French fashion. Contacts with France, which stood at the opposite side of the war front, were not only politically inadmissible, but also difficult due to heavy fighting. Although French fashion magazines continued to appear in Central Europe, especially through neutral Switzerland, French fashion was criticised for its inadequate luxury and impractical character.[98] The general inclination of fashion toward the Biedermeier style was considered to be an expression of the fashion style developed in Berlin and Vienna, which relied on the most famous chapters of German history as well as typical German national and folk costumes.[99] Olga Fastrová saw practical reasons behind the Biedermeier revival. She accused Paul Poiret of implementing fashion that bound ladies' legs with narrow skirts and even of forcing women to wear Oriental trousers. She proved that there is an unconscious relationship between war and women's skirts and that practical fashion would always prevail in war time.[100] However, as a matter of fact, constantly widening tunics

Nové Pařížské Mody, April 1915, p. 1.
Nové Pařížské Mody, February 1915, p. 2.

announced the arrival of Biedermeier fashion and wide skirts were often mentioned as an expected fashion feature even before the beginning of the First World War. On July 1, 1914 the magazine "Nové Pařížské Mody" mentioned that fashion of the Biedermeier style was being followed by American fashion magazines, although at that time it was complemented by long narrow skirts.

War caused a wave of patriotic and nationalistic emotions in all of the fighting states which were also reflected in efforts to seek a specifically national fashion. In Bohemia, these efforts were the peak of the folkloristic movement, whose origins date back to the 1880s. The movement continued through the organisation of the Ethnographic Exhibition in 1895 and ethnographic studies by the architect J. Koula which were used in preparation of the Czech exposition at the World Exhibition in Paris in 1900. The folkloristic movement also caused the foundation of the Ethnographic Museum and the association Zádruha in 1900. The aims of the Zádruha association were to further develop traditions of folk art and thus contribute to raising a feeling of Czech national identity as well as stimulating the further development of home industry. That is why the association gathered its own collection of patterns, especially through purchases of typical folk hand-made works, and produced its own new works — embroideries, laces, hand-made cloths and yarns, small parts of apparel, wooden toys, decorative Easter eggs, etc.[101] These circumstances gave rise to the idea of creating specifically Czech fashion that would rely on traditional types of folk costume.[102] Thus the so-called "peasant look" was created. However, Czech women did not take any action until the first months of the war when patriotic fee-

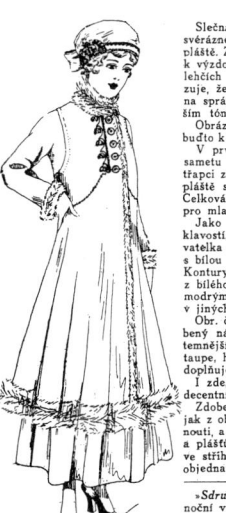

lings in the society emerged. The magazine "Ženské listy", which spoke for Czech female intelligentsia, claimed that "in the period of no visible fashion rule, when French fashion has lost its leading position... ...our, Czech fashion" should be created. This idea stood at the foundation of Sdružení pro svéráz krojový a povznesení českého domáckého průmyslu (Association for Czech National Costume and Development of Czech Home Industry) in March 1915. This association was established by Prague female designers and ladies from higher social circles, its chairperson being L. Bráfová-Riegrová. Its aims were to create its own works in the spirit of traditional Czech folk art, to gather materials necessary for studies of folk art, to collect old traditional techniques, patterns, and cuts. The association also paid considerable attention to social aspects — development of home industry and sales of its products should have provided means for suffering single housewives and their poor children. Among the members of the association were R. Tyršová, M. Teinitzerová, architects J. Koula and J. Fanta, Dr. V. Jiřík, F. A. Borovský, M. Suchardová, M. Suchardová-Brichová, O. Fastrová.

The first exhibition of the association was

Ženské listy 1915–1916

opened on May 8, 1915 at the exhibition halls of the Obecní dům (Municipal House). Besides retrospective dresses, 143 executed pieces and drawn designs for ladies' and children's clothing were exhibited.[103/] The exhibition attracted great attention; in her article in "Svéráz český", published by the Zádruha association from 1916, R. Tyršová praised the level of artistic feeling for folk costumes that female designers showed while working on designs, and the fact that folk costumes served as a basis not only for decoration, but also for patterns and the application of many interesting and appropriate motifs. Tyršová also claimed that individually designed and composed clothes were the Czech version of the so-called "artistic reformist clothes", which usually had somewhat clumsy, baggy cuts.

At the same time, Svaz českých spolků ženských (Union of Czech Ladies' Associations), headed by E. Machová, organised an exhibition that focused on the same theme at Václavské square no. 15. At this exhibition, the biggest awards were given to clothes from the M. Socháňová studio.

Another exhibition of national Czech apparel took place in the Náprstek Museum at Christmas 1915. The largest expositions at this sale exhibition belonged to associations Zádruha, Moravian Centre, and Slovak Lipa, Municipal Girls' Technical School in Prague, Women's Production Association, other schools, studios of M. Teinitzerová and A. Eckertová. Professor Koula, M. Aleš, and other well-known personalities also displayed their designs at the exhibition. Among the displayed pieces were not only works of textile and clothes, but also artistic items of all kinds including glass, ceramics, puppets, pieces of furniture, books, ironworks, etc. The ideas of Czech folkloristic movement quickly spread to the whole of Bohemia and Moravia — in 1916 similar exhibitions took place in Roudnice, Plzeň, Hořice, Příbram, Libochovice, Pardubice, Kolín, and other towns. In February and March 1916, the Exhibition of Czech Artistic Industry took place at Obecní dům in Prague, in which the Artěl association and Pražské umělecké dílny, among others, took part. Textile works did not have a significant display at this exhibition. Among exhibited items were works from textile workshop of Marie Teinitzerová, interior textiles by Vlasta Jelínková, designs for children's clothes by Anna Lukášová and Marie Kvěchová, blouse and collars by M. Dubovská. Dresses and photographs of ladies' costumes, executed according her own designs, were displayed only by Anna Boudová-Suchardová.

The most common way to create "peasant look"

Apparel in peasant look, Anna Boudová-Suchardová, 1915—1916.

was the use of a fashionable pattern complemented by decoration of folkloristic character. "Ženské listy" and "České Mody" regularly published designs by A. Dostálová, Ž. Felbrová, or B. Haunerová, whose patterns and decorations were inspired by traditional folk costume and at the same time they followed contemporary fashion tendencies. Designs by Z. Severová published by "Ženské listy" in June 1916 also met with positive acclaim. She linked elements of Czech national costumes with elements of the Biedermeier style. Interest in original folk costumes or their individual parts further increased during the last year of the First World War. Czech women also wore traditional folk costumes when they celebrated the foundation of the independent Czechoslovak state in October 1918.[104/]
The spreading of Czech folkloristic tendencies in fashion brought considerable differences in artistic quality of individual products and some even criticised the core of the national movement itself (Z. Wirth, F. X. Šalda, M. Jiránek). Pavel Janák considered a national movement in fashion to be an effort to create reformist apparel, but he was quite sceptical about its general spread as he thought it would be difficult for women to change the way they dressed without changing their lifestyle. National movements and folk costumes certainly played a significant role in raising the political and cultural awareness of Czech women. However, inspiration drawn from folk art was quite common in other European countries — for example, the top-quality Viennese tailor's workshop, Grünbaum, made fashion clothes decorated with Moravian embroidery, and workshops in Budapest produced pieces decorated with embroidered patterns derived from Slovak, Rumanian, and Transylvanian folk costumes.[105/]
Let us return now to the fashion designs pub-

Nové Pařížské Mody, February 1916, p. 11.

lished by fashion magazines. Autumn collections of 1915 further developed fashion tendencies that had appeared in the spring of the same year. Skirts were short and somewhat wider, widened at the waistline or below the hips, and sometimes pleated. The so-called frock-coats were short with bell-shaped tails, only for older ladies were they designed longer, they were 80—90 cm long. Blouses took on the shape of tailor's bodices, they reached only to or slightly below the waistline and they were complemented with bound sashes or bodice bands. Blouses were buttoned high up to the neck, and high turned collars and Stuart ruches were also popular. There also appeared collars prolonged at the back to form little hood. Winter outfits and cloaks were decorated with large fur collars or fur edgings,

Modní Svět, November 20, 1917, cover.
Modní Svět, June 5, 1917.

although for practical reasons they were fastened with press buttons so that they could be taken off and subsequently the outfit could have been worn as a spring or autumn piece. The shortages of war were also reflected in fashion — muffs became smaller and fur of lower quality was used for padding of cloth coats which replaced fur coats. Walking, social, and mourning dresses were made from taffeta and were decorated with pleats. Width of skirt was secured with braids inset to horizontal holes, which held the skirt in a somewhat raised position.

Spring and summer of 1916 witnessed tight-fitting bodices either of the princess cut or formed with overcasts, and also bell-shaped bodices and cloaks, which were loose at the waistline. They were complemented with high turned collars. Bowl-shaped folds and pockets, either forming cornets at the sides or inset to the side seams, appeared on skirts. Cloaks were either loose, bell-shaped, or loose at the back and bound at the front. Fashion magazines continued to recommend coat dress and the so-called "blouse" costumes (known today as skirt dress), complemented with a blouse or white collar and sleeves. The advantage of both types was that these dresses could have been made from older clothes. Since the time of Empire style, summer dresses had never been more subtle and tender than in the period of the First World War. They were made from light translucent materials — light linen, silk, batiste, and etamine — and decorated with subtle white or richelieu embroidery. Their dropped shoulders and rich skirts supported by wide underskirts with high embroidered flounce evoked the Biedermeier style, which was further emphasised by the shape of wide batiste collars of either wrapper or cape cut, embroidered with white, and three-quar-

Modní Svět, September 5,

ter sleeves with flounces. This character of contemporary summer dress was topped by the so-called "shepherd's" hats — wide straw hats decorated with flowers.

The name of the magazine "Nové Pařížské Mody" was changed to "Nové Mody" in April 1916. In summer, the magazine claimed that a considerably raised waistline and longer skirts were popular abroad. This tendency prevailed at spring 1917 collections in Vienna and Prague. The Empire cut of bodices was complemented by various shapes of arranged collars, which protruded away from the neck. The skirt was still quite wide at the beginning, but gradually, over the course of several weeks, it became longer and tighter, and it gained a straight silhouette. A one-piece dress appeared with loose band or sash above the waistline. This dress often had bowl-shaped folds or pockets on the sides. New blouses also had a similar cut: they were straight and loose, reaching below hips and were fitted with a band above the waistline. Blouses were also made in the form of an over-blouse without fastening. Furthermore, embroidered white etamine blouses were also popular in the Czech lands.

Costumes lost their tails and wide skirts. Once again, a tight-fitting English cut with narrow skirt came into fashion. A narrow skirt was recommended for its little use of material. However, even such skirts became too luxurious for Czech women by the fourth year of the war, as there was a serious lack of quality material. Consequently, cheaper replacements began to be used, such as stinging-nettle fabrics — which were produced in Broumov, Králíky, Kerhartice n. Orlicí, and other places in Bohemia — and the so-called "textilosa" — a paper pulp combined with natural, especially hemp, fabric. Designers also sought alterna-

Modní Svět, April 20, 1918.

tives for valuable materials: they used hop tendrils and threads of bast of Genista Dalmatica.[106] Fashion reflected the shortages of war in combinations of various materials, patterns, and cuts. However, there were also serious problems with sewing threads as their price increased from 60 hallers (price before the war) to 14 crowns.[107] In "Ženské listy", a magazine published by Ženský výrobní spolek, fashion articles were gradually replaced by sad stories describing sufferings of Czech women. The Viennese magazine "Modní Svět", which was published in a Czech language version, helped women to solve problems of their apparel. From the beginning of the war, the magazine regularly published a column called "Practical Home Sewing" as well as detailed instructions for adaptation of old clothes into new models. However, it is

Modní Svět, May 20, 1918.

quite strange that even a two year old dress was considered to be old.

Despite shortage of fabrics, "Modní Svět" and "Nové Mody" continued to capture the quickly-developing fashion of the period. In the summer of 1917, latest fashion novelty was a skirt with gathered folds at the bottom "in a Turkish way". It was longer, whirred at the bottom and gathered into a narrower or wider band of cloth. Although this cut did not become very common, even loose skirts were slightly whirred at the bottom edge and sometimes decorated with an embroidered line. During 1918 skirts of evening dresses were enriched with variously arranged tunics and folds which emphasised the line of the hips. Skirts were complemented with vest bodices or blouses with tails at the front and prolonged belt, as well as various forms of loose long blouses with or without sleeves. Open loose cloaks of various lengths were made from light materials. In this period, coat dresses and one-piece dresses still continued to be popular.

The period of the First World War is represented in the collection of the Museum of Decorative Arts in Prague by only a small number of clothes which, however, perfectly document the development of fashion and the difficulties it had to undertake during the war. A luxurious example of "tunic" fashion is a wedding dress of white crepe-de-Chine and lace (inv. no. 73 610) made by the Maison Šesták on Spálená street in Prague. Made in 1915, the dress has a kimono bodice gathered at the waist and a tunic skirt with three arranged flounces. The influence of the Biedermeier style can be traced in a costume dress of black taffeta (inv. no. 69 254). This dress was made by an unknown fashion house around 1915. It has a single rounded tail at the back, a skirt with three flounces, decorated with pleated edges and rows of buttons. A half-length dress of black taffeta (inv. no. 69 077) with puff sleeves, boat neckline with flat collar, and a skirt decorated with folds and edgings serves as an example of fashion production mentioned by Růžena Tillnerová in 1916, when she wrote that Prague was full of black taffeta dresses.[108/]

White embroidered dresses are also represented with two pieces in the collection of the Museum of Decorative Arts. The first dress originates from Moravia (inv. no. 65 855) and it has long and wide "fichu" collar and a skirt decorated with rows of whirred folds at the waistline. The second dress comes from an unknown fashion house (inv. no. 57 727) and it has long shawl collar reaching the waistline and skirt widened with three flounces. New straight silhouette is represented in the collection of the Museum of Decorative Arts by a girl's Confirmation dress from the František

Fashion between 1915 and 1918

< Girl's Confirmation Dress, embroidered silk, Prague, František Matějovský 1917, inv. no. 73 606.

Girl's Dress
embroidered etamine,
Moravia 1916, inv. no. 65 855.

Ladies' Formal Dress
black silk with brocaded pattern, probably Prague,
around 1918, inv. no. 82 375.

Matějovský fashion workshop in Prague. The dress (inv. no. 73 606), made in 1917, has a shortened bodice covered with straight lace bolero, and a pleated skirt girded with a wide ribbon below the breasts. The last phase of war fashion is represented by a dress of black georgette with bunches of violet and yellow roses (inv. no. 82 375). The dress has a straight silhouette with a kimono-bolero bodice, whose crossed front parts change into ribbons tied at the back. A skirt with a tunic at the back is decorated with bowl-shaped folds on the sides. This dress allegedly originates from an unknown fashion workshop in Prague. A luxurious evening dress of turquoise-blue satin and tulle (inv. no. 70 244) has an extraordinarily simple and inventive cut. It features a tunic skirt arranged from a band of spirally twisted fabric sewn into a point on one side, and it is complemented by a bodice with crossed front and back parts. The dress (inv. no. 70 244) is marked with a company sticker "E. Roubitček Prag" (Arnoštka Roubíčková) and, judging by its design, it originates from 1918 — 1919.

Fashion influenced by national folk costume is represented by several blouses and two-piece white linen, and white embroidered dresses, as well as by a coat from hand-woven woollen fabric of peach colour with woven blue-violet stylised floral ornament. It is of an Empire cut with shortened bodice and bell-shaped skirt. A small stand-up collar and cuffs are decorated with sheep fur. The hem was probably also decorated with fur, but it was later altered. This coat was made by Marie Teinitzerová (1879—1960), one of the founders of modern Czech textile production, who only rarely designed clothes. The coat originates from the period when Teinitzerová already had her own workshop in Jindřichův Hradec and her own shop in Prague. She took part in the activities of the Artěl association and she also took part in group exhibitions of artists influenced by the national folkloristic movement. In December 1916 she organised her solo exhibition at the Museum of Decorative Arts in Prague, where she exhibited, among other pieces, several clothes. This coat is very similar in its cut and decoration to the design published by Anna Dostálová in "Ženské listy" in December 1915.

Isolation resulting from the war and difficulties connected with travelling made it impossible to buy clothes in Vienna and elsewhere abroad as was common for members of the wealthiest part of society in Bohemia. This fact contributed to the quick development of several Prague fashion houses. The most important fashion enterprise in Prague during the First World War was the Arnoštka Roubíčková fashion house. Although Arnoštka began to build her fashion house in her later years, she not only learnt how to quickly and surely follow fashion trends and professional affairs, but she also managed to create an elegant and cultivated environment in her fashion house, which was known for its personal approach to every customer. Arnoštka moved to Prague from Kralovice in Western Bohemia. She married Julius Roubíček, a tradesman in Hungarian corn. In 1896 she gave birth to her daughter Helena and soon afterwards also to her other children, Josef and Adéla. She divorced in 1911 and subsequent existential problems brought her to the decision to establish her own fashion house. She learnt sewing with an unknown seamstress, her neighbour in Nekázanka street, where she and her children lived after the divorce. She had already visited Paris several times before the beginning of the First World War, however, she did not have enough money to

Woollen coat with woven pattern in peasant look, Jindřichův Hradec, M. Teinitzerová, 1915-1916, inv. no. 89 576.

Dámské Akademické Modní Listy,
March 20, 1915.

visit fashion shows, so she went to horse races where she could see latest tendencies of world fashion worn by Parisian ladies. She also brought fabrics for her own models from Paris. She purchased off-cuts for discount prices, which she managed to use and combine after she came home. Arnoštka Roubíčková was very wise and made herself a large stock of fabrics before the war. Consequently, she was not hit by shortages of the war. Her company developed quickly and successfully and in 1916 she moved, together with her family and entire workshop, to the luxurious newly constructed Palace Koruna on the corner of Václavské Square and Příkopy. She also employed her two daughters who received top-quality education abroad before the war. Helena worked as an accountant and was in charge of the customers' department, while

Ada created and drew designs. Arnoštka Roubíčková soon gained the wealthiest Prague clientele of Czech, German, and Jewish origin, she made clothes for members of the aristocracy, for wives of bankers and entrepreneurs, and for actresses.[109/] Her fashion house also made a number of costumes for theatre plays and feature films.

Around 1915, Hana Podolská with her fashion house became a competitor to Arnoštka Roubíčková. A daughter of the Prague architect Vošahlík, Podolská trained for a seamstress in order to help feed her brothers and sisters after her father's untimely death. After her marriage to the painter Viktor Podolski she opened her own workshop which she enlarged and improved after she had gained a luxurious apartment on the fourth floor of the Lucerna Palace.[110/] The foundation of the Hana Podolská fashion house was announced in "Český svět" and complemented by a number of advertisements in Czech, both fashion and social, press. Hana Podolská focused primarily on Czech customers and, by the end of the war, she succeeded in building a significant number of Czech clientele. Her activities fully developed after 1918.

One of another important Prague fashion leaders, Oldřich Rosenbaum, also began his career during the war years. He grew up and trained at the workshop of his mother Eliška at no. 53 Štěpánská Street in Prague II. In 1907, the Prague directory included this workshop among producers of ready-made clothes, but in 1910, it was already advertised as a ladies' fashion house.[111/] A number of other fashion houses participated in Prague fashion production during the First World War. One of them was the company "Moritz Schiller, trader of fashion, silk, and woollen clothes and fabrics", which produced ready-made clothes as well as those made to order. Its owners, Rudolf and Bedřich Schillers, regularly visited fashion shows in Paris before the First World War. They were usually accompanied by the directrice of their enterprise, Josefa Weigertová, formerly employed by the Zwieback fashion house in Vienna. Later she ran her own fashion house at Spálená Street.[112/] Josefa Weigertová also helped Marie Teinitzerová with preparation of her exhibition in 1916.[113/] This generation of young fashion designers, whose activities during the First World War are only partially known, fully proved its qualities immediately after the end of the war in 1918. The foundation, finally, of a new, original Czech fashion magazine, "Moda a vkus" in 1919 was a result of collaboration of female fashion designers who promoted peasant look during the war. Even the association Pražská Moda, which was established in 1920 and sought to form, create, and protect the phenomenon of Prague fashion, united fashion designers who had already been active during the war. After the war, companies such as Podolská, Rosenbaum, and Roubíčková, influenced by their French counterparts, changed into luxurious modelling fashion houses. Continuing the activities of previous generations, relying on top-quality tailoring tradition, with new social orders resulting from the foundation of the independent Czechoslovak state, Czech fashion creation would reach its outstanding quality in the period between the two world wars.

Módní atelier pro dámy
H. Podolské
Nejnovější zimní novinky
a modely v repres. skladě
Praha II.,
Vodičkova ul., palác „Lucerna".

Nové Mody, July 1916, p. 9.

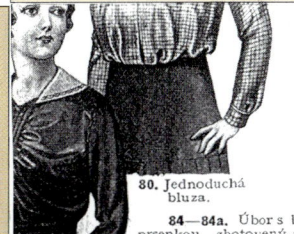

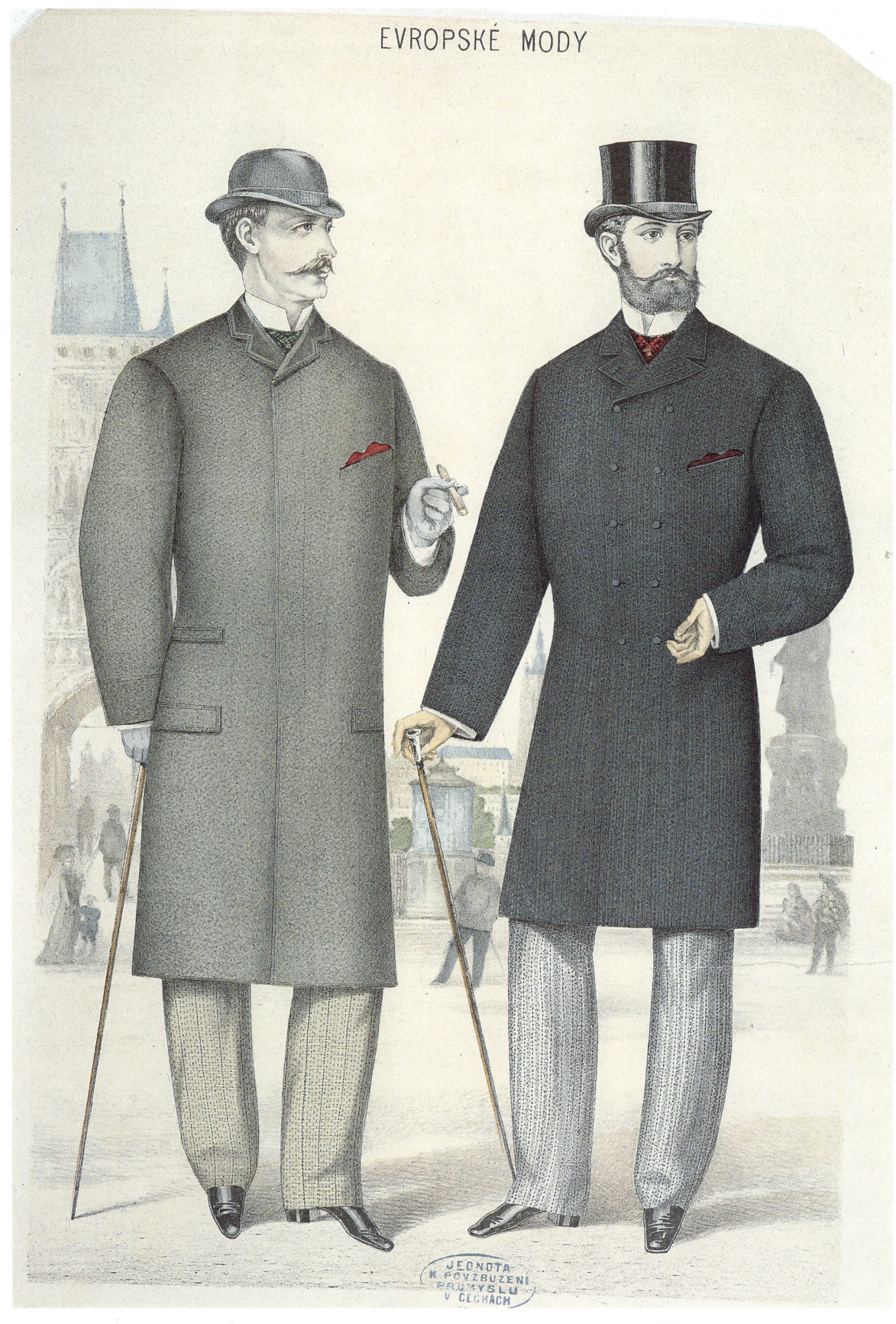

Evropské Mody,
September
1883.

MEN'S fashion

At the beginning of the period in question, men's fashion had linked on rich and significant tradition.[114/] During the 19th century, Czech tailors, like others in Europe, sought solutions to technological problems, especially construction of patterns. New knowledge was spread by individual publications as well as by special magazines ("Ročenka pro hotovitele mužského oděvu", Prague 1845 — probably 1847, and "Modní list pro hotovitele mužského oděvu", Prague 1850 - 1856, published by Václav Huttar; and "Zlaté dno", published by Vojtěch Čihař). Tailors from all regions of Bohemia contributed their patterns to these publications. Literally the entire nation took part in creating a special type of apparel, which was to express the political ambitions of Czech society in the stormy year of 1848. This dress was based on contemporary city wear complemented with specific details, especially fastening with braids. The dress was first used on uniforms of the newly established institutions including Svornost, Národní obrana, and Studentská akademická legie. Later, this dress developed into a universal patriotic men's coat — a chamarre.[115/] The chamarre was used as a symbol of democratic patriotic Czech society from 1850 till the end of the 19th century. Although wearing a chamarre was forbidden after the victory of Austrian absolutism in 1851, they appeared again at the beginning of the 1860s on various public social occasions. Even the famous composer Bedřich Smetana wore a chamarre on the occasion of the ceremonial opening of the National Theatre in June 1881, in which Prince Rudolf of Hapsburg also took part.[116/]

The second half of the 19th century was marked by a significant development of tailor's workshops and fashion houses, which was reflected by outstanding international successes. Especially the firm of Erasmus and Robert Krach regularly took part in international exhibitions from 1845, including the Provincial Exhibition in Vienna in 1845, and exhibitions in London in 1851, New York in 1853, Munich in 1854, Paris in 1855, and in London in 1862. The company received many awards and prizes at these events. In 1858 the firm opened its branch in Vienna and many members of the Viennese court and high aristocracy became its customers. At the same time, the company continued to produce ready-made clothes as well as large numbers of various uniforms.[117/] Robert Krach became a recognised and well-respected specialist both in Bohemia and abroad. He received the French Order of the Legion of Honour and was an active member of several economic institutions.[118/] Successful development of the firm was halted by the untimely death of Robert Krach in January 1868, several months before his 50th birthday. Although his brother Erasmus managed the fashion house in Prague for many years to come, the firm's activities were quite limited.[119/]

After the death of Robert Krach, the leading position among Czech men's tailors was taken by the company Matyáše Mottla synové, established in the 1850s. The firm was managed by brothers Vendelín and Alois Mottl. It developed successfully and continued to spread the good reputation of Czech tailor's abroad. It displayed its products at a number of international exhibitions, including exhibitions in Paris in 1867, Vienna in 1873, Philadelphia in 1876, and in Paris in 1878. At this exhibition, Vendelín Mottl was appointed a member of the jury. The Mottl brothers received numerous awards and prizes.

The Mottl brothers focused their considerable attention on technical and technological aspects of fashion production. As a manager of the company, Vendelín Mottl began to publish his pattern drawings for various clothes in Czech and foreign magazines already during the 1850s. Later he was asked by Jednota ku povzbuzení průmyslu v Čechách to publish a book based on his experience. Thus a comprehensive publication "Umění přistřihačské" (The Art of Cutting) was created, in which he described theoretical aspects of cutting in detail and published many drawings concerning fashion design. The first edition came out in 1892 and a second enlarged edition was published in 1897. New types of fabrics for suits were made according to his designs and he also held several dozen various patents and privileges. He was an active collaborator in the European Fashion Academy in Dresden, which awarded him a silver and, later, also gold medal, and appointed him a chairman of its senate. He also became a royal and imperial court supplier and received various

honours. His high position among Prague entrepreneurs resulted in a silver medal of the City of Prague and Silver Medal of Merit of Jednota ku povzbuzení průmyslu v Čechách.[120]

The Mottl brothers were not the only tailors in Bohemia who focused on the technical aspects of fashion production. In 1884, Prague tailor Josef Michalík, publisher of the magazine "Evropské Mody", published a booklet with the title "Odborné vědomosti pro mužské krejčí" (Special Knowledge of Tailor). The establishment of the První akademie krejčovská v Praze in 1894 also had a great significance for spreading knowledge concerning the tailoring craft. The academy was founded by Jan Kratina after he had spent

Picture supplement of Zlaté dno 1871, no. 1.

many years at cutting schools abroad. This Prague tailor taught the art of cutting according his own cuts. During the following decades, Kratina's academy educated thousands of students and published several editions of its own practical manuals such as "Kniha mužských střihů", "Kniha dámských střihů", and "Kniha moderního prádla". In addition, the academy also published both men's and ladies' fashion magazines that were focused on the French fashion style.[121/]

Contemporary fashion production was regularly displayed at great economic exhibitions. The biggest event of this kind was the Anniversary Regional Exhibition in Prague in 1891 which was organised on the occasion of the 100th anniversary of the first industrial exhibition that took place in Klementinum in Prague in 1791. The influence of Vendelín Mottl was reflected by his appointment to the general jury of the exhibition. He became the chairman of the jury of the of seventh group, dedicated to fashion. His fashion house presented itself to the Czech public with an extensive selection of perfect suits of all kinds: evening suits, suits for walks, various uniforms, sport clothing, clothing for hunting, clothes for tennis and croquette. The chamarre was also among the exhibited items. The display of the Mottl fashion house held a honorary position at the entrance pavilion. It was surrounded by display cases of other famous Prague tailors' workshops including Alois Vavruška, a specialist in men's clothes and uniforms, and Jan Beneš, whose firm displayed ladies' clothes with great spectacle. A lady on a horse wore a black riding costume, an amazon in a red frock-coat stood beside her, and a ladies' dress of green cloth was arranged on the opposite side of the display.[122/]

Another great exhibition of fashion production in Prague was the Anniversary Exhibition of the Prague Chamber of Trade and Commerce, organised in 1908 on the occasion of the 50th anniversary of the rule of the Emperor Franz Joseph. Clothes were presented under the names of individual firms or associations (Společenstvo krejčí staroměstských, novoměstských a malostranských), some of them were also presented as part of the so-called "artistically arranged interiors", in which firms producing men's and ladies' clothes combined their display, also complemented by modelling firms, furriers, firms producing underwear, blouses, etc. Firms combined their products, arranged their clothes on mannequins, and thus created scenes from social, family, and sport life. For example, Josef Kříž and Marie Tichá presented their beach apparel, František Krejčí, Imperial and Royal tailor for men and women, created a scene from his own fashion house, men's tailor Augustin Čermák and ladies' tailor Karel Čermák created a sports scene in a park. A stage design of this exposition was made by the sculptor, professor Ludvík Wurzel.[123]

Much space in the catalogue of the Prague exhibition was devoted to the production of men's underwear which, during the 19th century, became an important export goods of the Austro-Hungarian Empire. Men's shirts, collars, cuffs, underwear, and handkerchiefs of cheap, middle, and fashionable quality were exported from Bohemia to the entire world with the exception of British markets. The largest supplier was the firm Joss and Löwenstein with its headquarters in Prague 7, branches in Klatovy, Nýřany, and Vimperk, and stores in Paris, Rio de Janeiro, Oslo, Trieste, Vienna, and Budapest.

Besides pieces made for individual customers by their specific order, a number of fashion houses also produced ready-made clothes. The former was a question of a prestige, the latter undoubtedly supported firms' economic prosperity. Today we can hardly judge the amount of ready-made clothes produced. For example, the firm Františka a Vlad. Zvolský at Smíchov in Prague not only made clothes by order, but also maintained its own warehouse of equipment for the Sokol association as well as various kinds of apparel — civilians', military, clerks', and guilds' uniforms. A fashion house with production focused on ready-made clothes alone was founded by Zikmund Stránský in 1888: it produced all kinds of top quality clothes for men and boys on a large scale.[125]

The town of Prostějov in Moravia became an important centre for the large-scale production of ready-made clothes. In 1858, Moritz Mandl, the local trader, organiser, and master of tailors' guild received a licence for "large-scale production of all kinds of men's apparel". Gradually he produced not only cheap ready-made clothes from average materials, but also ready-made clothes from better quality fabrics which were exported and later sold to members of mid and high society. In 1872, his factory employed 120 workers, but it also contracted the services of several hundred of the labour force of the entire region. Mandl's success, close distance to Vienna, and cheap labour force were the main factors that allowed Prostějov to gradually became an important centre of ready-made clothes production. The Viennese firm Tiring also opened its production branches in Prostějov and in 1873 Joachim Pollak also commenced his successful entrepreneurial activities in the field of men's fashion in the region. In the following year,

ZÁŘÍ 1882

EVROPSKÉ MODY
Administrace Ferd. třída
PRAHA

ČERVEN 1884.

EVROPSKÉ MODY
Administrace Jungm. třída 5.
PRAHA

David Schwarzmann opened his workshop in Prostějov and in 1876 he was followed by another two entrepreneurs: Herman Berger and A. Zentner & Sohn. These and other large producers of ready-made clothes exported their products — especially men's and ladies' ready-made clothes — to Russia, Turkey, and to the Balkans, and, starting in the 1880s, also to Egypt, Australia, and North America. During the First World War, the company shifted its attention from production of normal ready-made clothes to the production of military uniforms.[126/]

Let us have a closer look at changes of men's apparel in Bohemia in the period between 1870—1918. The 1870s did not witness any significant changes in men's fashion. On the contrary, in 1870 the fashion magazine "Zlaté dno" mentioned that the contemporary fashion had not changed for several years and that only general taste became more refined.[127/] The warmest piece of clothing was a fur-coat, which regularly appeared on pages of winter issues of fashion magazines. Winter-coats were made from thick, "bushy" materials, and they featured either single- or double-breasted fastening. They were buttoned high up to the neck. The less warm type of winter-coats were overcoats — winter, spring, and summer — with both single- and double-breasted buttoning. Another type was a so-called "paletot" — lighter and shorter half-tight fitting coats. All kinds of cloaks were decorated with edging of wide silk ribbon, in case of thinner materials, the lapels and collars were made of back-stitched satin. Collars of winter-coats were covered with velvet in order to increase flexibility.

Around 1870, jackets and trousers of men's suits were still usually made from different materials, although suits made completely from one type of fabric appeared on pages of fashion magazines already during the 1860s.

The first suit (a hunting suit) made from one type of fabric was published by the magazine "Erinnerungen" in Prague in 1850.[128/] In April 1871 such a suit was designed for "regular walks". The coat took either the form of a tight-fitting cutaway, which was very popular at that time, or a jacket. A cutaway was a tight-fitting coat with long tails, and with long lapels or a shawl collar. At that period, it was usually designed to have a somewhat lowered waistline. The front parts were cut diagonally toward the lower edge, and the back parts featured a slit. A jacket differed from a cutaway by having a looser cut and also shorter length. It was designed for sport, trips, and walks; when worn over a padded waistcoat, it was also used for "a short walk across the street".[129/]

A suit for social occasions was a cutaway or a black coat with the front and back parts cut straight. In 1868, it was considered to be "democratic" and was highly recommended as a replacement for the aristocratic frock-coat.[130/] Despite efforts to use a tail-coat only for official social occasions, as we mentioned at the beginning of this book, it gained positions at Národní Beseda balls where it pushed away a chamarre. Until the end of the 19th century a chamarre was considered to be a symbol of patriotic feelings. In the 1870s, fastening with braids was also used on other types of men's coats, which were regarded as "Slavic". Waistcoats were made from the same material as jackets and trousers, and they featured single-breasted and increasingly more often also double-breasted fastening.

In April 1869, the fashion in Paris spoke for tight-fitting trousers, but in England trousers were worn straight, i.e. more comfortable. Although the cuts that appeared in "Zlaté dno" also inclined toward more comfortable trousers, in December 1870 the fashion magazines

began to publish designs of tight-fitting trousers. In 1869, trousers were made with stripes on the sides, but in 1871 these became either very narrow or were completely abandoned. By the end of the century, men's fashion became even more specialised and its forms became more refined. Types of top coats remained the same and paletots, suitable for walks and sport occasions, were still in favour. In 1899, a paletot for sport had a straight cut and reached the level of the knees. It featured a velvet collar, and slashed pockets with flaps. Paletots for sport gained a new form — the so-called "Ulster" coat appeared on the scene. The Ulster was an overcoat which served to substitute a fur-coat. It was characterised by front fastening for the entire length of the coat, a high collar, and numerous pockets.[131/]
Similarly as in the previous period, suits had a coat in the form of a jacket or a cutaway. Cutaways were used on the street and for walks, and they could also be used for social occasions. They were mostly fastened with three buttons, the front parts were diagonally cut, and were either straight or rounded at the bottom. There was a vent at the back. The cuts of jackets differed according to their function. A double-breasted fastening was used for sports, and single-breasted fastening for "common home or street dress".[132/] The popularity of jackets was continually on the increase — in September 1899 they were regarded as the most comfortable and practical dress for work and in 1902 the fashion magazine "Elegantní kroj" stated that "the jacket had become popular dress".[133/] Trousers were narrowing towards the bottom.

The coat, unofficially known under the German term "kaiserrock", held an important position in men's fashion. It was used for walks and was cut at or a little below the knees, fastened with four buttons and was made up from dark-grey material for winter and light coloured material for summer. Its formal variation was shorter and cut approximately five centimetres above the knees. It was made up from black material, fastened with three buttons, and its revers were covered with silk. It was worn done up with black trousers. For home occasions it was worn open with lightweight waistcoat and grey striped trousers.

A tail-coat was reserved only for large formal occasions such as ceremonial concerts, family celebrations, meals in restaurants or on steamboats, and other evening "dinner" occasions. At the beginning of the 20th century, a dinner-suit came from England to Bohemia[134/] and was worn for less formal occasions. Its use was questioned at the beginning, but around 1910 it was generally accepted by the public.[135/]

Around 1910, fashion magazines published reviews of not only basic dress, but they also concentrated on hats, shirts, ties, material and kind of shoes, colour of tights, and kind of handkerchiefs. The press dealt with such problems as whether to wear long pants and short socks or short pants and stockings up to the knees, how to use false shirt-fronts and collars, and whether to use a tight or fastened stock. Etiquette in men's fashion became stricter throughout the years.[136/] Types of men's apparel were stabilised according to the demands of modern society and they remained practically unchanged until the present day.

Evropské Mody,
December
1892.

| Ochranné zvláštnosti francouzské, nejnovější a nejlepší **pro pány i dámy** zvláštní oddělení firmy: Emanuel Binoveo, drogerie, Praha, Poříč 21. Brožovaný ceník zdarma. | **JOSEF ŠPRINGL,** závod obuvnický Praha II., Vodičkova ul. č. 6. »u Hopfenštoků.« Moderní výroba všech druhů obuvi dle mody anglické francouzské atd. Vhodné ceny. Elegantní úprava. Založeno roku 1885. |

| Největší továrna toho druhu v Čechách, na Moravě a ve Slezsku. |  | Továrna v Brně, Cejl, číslo 38. Telefon 576 a 219. |

C. a k. dvorní dodavatel. **ZIKMUND FLUSS V PRAZE.** Komorní dodavatel.

Hlavní sklad Václavské náměstí číslo 52 nové, vedle Primasů.
Tovární sklad: Malá Strana, Mostecká ulice 40 v domě Záložny.

Specialita Barvení pštrosích per.   Specialita: Barvení hedv. toilet všech barev.
11 zlatými medailemi vyznamenaná
C. a k. dvorní barvírna a chemická prádelna
(pomocí páry a strojů) pro šatstvo pánů, dam i dítek, buď v celosti neb rozpárané, uniformy, látky nábytkové, koberce, záclony, plyše, aksamity, vějíře z per, pravé krajky atd.
Zakázky venkovské vyřizují se rychle a správně.

Anglické kostýmy zhotovuje z pravých angl. látek JOS. ŠÍD PRAHA-II., Havlíčkova býv. Jezdecká ul. číslo 8. I. patro.

Epilogue

The best materials researching the history of clothing are the clothes themselves. The selection of fabric, the specific cut, traces of careful mending and alterations, the number and type of decorative accessores and support construction such as bone, hoops, yokes, applied bodices, padding and filling, used to create a contemporary fashionable silhouette — all of this provides a better picture of many generations of men and women tha dozens of portraits and photographs. The first impulse for the creation of this publication was the extensive collection of clothes in the Museum of Decorative Arts in Prague, which came into existence as part of the department of textiles. The museum, founded by the Chamber of Trade and Commerce in 1885, did not show any big interest in clothes at the beginning it focused its attention on collecting other items of textile production. The clothes collection began to grow after the Museum acquired the greater part of the funds of the Museum of Fashion in Jemniště which ceased to exist in 1962. Since then it has been systematically enlarged by purchases and gifts from private parties and the museum also documents contemporary fashion production.

Great impulses for the existence of the clothes collection were very successful exhibitions of fashion products — "150 Years of Czech Fashion" organised in 1960, and "Woman of Art Nouveau Period" organised in 1976. These events were later followed by a series of exhibitions known under the title "From the Waltz to the Tango". The first part covered period between 1780—1870 and took place in 1989, the second part covered the period from 1870 to 1914 and was organised in 1994. Another exhibition "Elegance of the First Republic" showed fashion products from the period 1918—1939 and took place in 1996.

In connection with the last exhibition, the Olympia publishing house with the support of the Museum of Decorative Arts decided to publish a series of books on Czech fashion, the first volume of which was published as a catalogue of the exhibition "Elegance of the First Republic". Now there comes another volume, which is a revised and enlarged version of the catalogue of the exhibition "From the Waltz to the Tango II — Czech Fashion 1870—1914". This book contains an essay concerning the period of the First World War, which was not included in the original exhibition, and it also features a revised essay by Milena Zeminová concerning Prague tailors' workshops, which originally dealt with the development of tailors' production during the entire 19th century, while this publication deals with the period starting in the 1870s. Individual chapters contain allusions to the collection of the Museum of Decorative Arts, which complement information regarding the development of fashion as well as reveal the richness and quality of the museum's clothing collection.

The preparation of this enlarged edition took place with the support of the Research Support Scheme of the Open Society Institute (Grant No. 102/1996) and in collaboration with the employees of the State Library, to whom I am grateful for research in many contemporary magazines. I am especially grateful to colleagues from the textile and graphic departments as well as from the library of the Museum of Decorative Arts for their help, advice, and cooperation.

Notes

1/ Almanach Národní Besedy. Praha 1908, pp. 21—72.
2/ Almanach Národní Besedy. Praha 1908, p. 42.
3/ Almanach Národní Besedy. Praha 1908, p. 45.
4/ Almanach Národní Besedy. Praha 1908, p. 44.
5/ Almanach Národní Besedy. Praha 1908, p. 56.
6/ Katalog pavillonu Král. hl. m. Prahy a odborných skupin městských na výstavě Obchodní a živnostenské komory Pražské... Prague 1908, pp. 23—25; Konečná, H., Kopecký, J.: Čtení o Národním divadle. Prague 1984, from p. 15.
7/ Konečná, H., l. c., from p. 18.
8/ Konečná, H., l. c., from p. 30.
9/ Neruda, J.: Fejeton. Zlatá Praha, 1, 1884 no. 3, p. 39.
10/ Konečná, H., l. c., p. 54.
11/ Javorin, A.: Pražské arény. Prague 1958, from p. 31.
12/ Katalog pavillonu... Prague 1908, l. c., pp. 25, 29.
13/ Mathesy, F.: Pohledy ze Staré Prahy. Prague 1946, p. 94.
14/ Světozor, 25, 1891, no. 26, p. 302, no. 48, p. 571, no. 49, p. 586.
15/ Allgemeine Landes — Ausstellung in Prag... Hauptkatalog. Prague 1891, from p. 119.
16/ Katalog pavillonu... Prague 1908, p. 40.
17/ Pechová-Krásnohorská, E.: Co přinesla léta. Part II. vol. 1. Prague 1928, p. 146.
18/ Jubilejní výstava obvodu Obchodní a živnostenské komory v Praze 1908. Ústřední skupin. katalog č. 1., Praha 1908, from p. 300.
19/ Almanach Národní Besedy. Prague 1908, p. 71.
20/ Katalog pavillonu... Prague 1908, p. 62.
21/ Pacina, V.: Sport v Království českém. Prague 1986, from p. 125.
22/ Pacina, V.: Sport v Království českém. Prague 1986, p. 197.
23/ Katalog pavillonu... Prague 1908, p. 136.
24/ Vydrová, J.: Žena doby secese. (Catalogue). Prague, Museum of Decorative Arts 1980, unpaginated
25/ Český svět, 1, 1905 no. 19, pp. 143—144
26/ Český svět, 10, 1914 no. 24, p. 6; no. 37, unpaginated, no. 21, no. 20, pp. 20—21; no. 23, pp. 18—19.
27/ Potocká, J.: Snahy o reformu manželství. In: Boudoir, dámám a dívkám, compiled by O. Fastrová. Prague 1914, p. 106.
28/ Janko, J. — Štrbáňová, S.: Věda Purkyňovy doby. Prague 1988, from p. 243.
29/ Ottův slovník naučný. vol. 27. Entry: Ženská emancipace. Prague 1908, from p. 810
30/ Pechová-Krásnohorská, E., l. c., part II, vol. 2, from p. 133. (The first editor of Ženské listy was Věnceslava Lužická-Srbová).
31/ Statistická knížka král. hl. m. Prahy... 1881. Part I Prague 1882, p. 197.
32/ Ottův slovník naučný, l. c., from p. 810.
33/ Pechová-Krásnohorská, E.: l. c.,Part II, vol. 1, from p. 120
34/ Ottův slovník naučný, l. c., p. 811.
35/ Český svět, 2, 1906 no. 7, unpaginated.
36/ Pechová-Krásnohorská, E., l. c., Part II, vol. 1, p. 144.
37/ Nevšímalová, K.: O volebním právu žen. Ženské listy 1906, p. 221.
38/ Vítková, M.: F. Plamínková — průkopnice politického hnutí. In: Kniha o životě, práci a osobnosti F. Plamínkové. Prague 1935, from p. 197.
39/ Katalog pavillonu... Praha 1908, from p. 63.
40/ Potocká, J., l. c., p. 107.
41/ Etiketa v toilettách. Nové Pařížské Mody, 1907, no. 23, p. 1.
42/ Nové Pařížské Mody, 1908 no. 3, pp. 3—4.
43/ Nové Pařížské Mody, 1908 no. 20, pp. 1—2.
44/ Nové Pařížské Mody, 1908 no. 2, pp. 1—2.
45/ Bazar, 20, 1890 no. 24, p. 153.
46/ Bazar, 24, 1894 no. 20, p. 155.
47/ Květ, J.: Jak soudí lékař o toilettě dámy. Pařížské Mody, 1, 1894 no. 5, p. 99 (first part), no. 6, p. 124 (second part), no. 7, p. 147 (third part).
48/ Vydrová, J., l. c., unpaginated.
49/ Statistická knížka král. hl. m. Prahy... 1881. Part I. Prague 1882, from p. 90.
50/ Adresář král. hl. m. Prahy a sousedních obcí... Prague 1896, pp. 90, 97, 134, 133.
51/ Adresář král. hl. m. Prahy a obcí sousedních... Praha 1910, pp. 152, 165, 457, 141, 20, 392, 230.
52/ Benda, J.: Oděvní průmysl v českých zemích. Part I. In: Z dějin textilu. Suppl. 2, Ústí nad Orlicí 1984, p. 62.
53/ Světozor, 4, 1870 no. 9, p. 68; Šimoníková, M.:

[54] První pražský obchodní dům. Umění a řemesla, 1988, no. 1, from p. 36.
[54] Pražský Bon Marché. Český svět, 1, 1904 no. 3, from p. 124.
[55] Buxbaum, G.: Mode aus Wien. Vienna 1986, p. 359.
[56] Pechová-Krásnohorská, E., l. c., Part II, vol. 2, p. 150.
[57] Brožová, J.: Z počátků českého módního obrázku. Věci a lidé, 5, 1953—54, from p. 474.
[58] Bazar, 27, 1897 no. 7, pp. 49; 25, 1895 no. 12, p. 89; no. 19, p. 145.
[59] Bazar, 24, 1894 no. 6, p. 50.
[60] Jílková, J.: Soupis textilních časopisů a ročenek v českých zemích v letech 1787—1982. In: Z dějin textilu. Studie a materiály. vol. 4. Ústí nad Orlicí 1983.
[61] Rozmarná, B.: Módní žurnály. Ženské listy, 6, 1878 no. 1, from p. 7.
[62] Neruda, J.: Milé Týnynce. (Feature column from 15 June 1884). In: Drobné klepy. Prague 1911, p. 53.
[63] Pařížské Mody, 1, 1894 no.. 8, p. 167.
[64] Český svět, 1, 1905 no. 18, p. 120.
[65] Vydrová, J., l. c., unpaginated.
[66] Brožová, J.: Historismus. Umělecké řemeslo 1860—1900. (Catalogue). Museum of Decorative Arts Praha 1975—1976, unpaginated.
I thank to PhDr. Jarmila Brožová for her comments, above all on the section of historicism.
[67] Bazar, 29, 1899 no. 21, p. 161.
[68] Bazar, 22, 1892 no. 8, p. 57.
[69] Uchalová, E.: Od valčíku po tango. Part I, Česká móda 1780—1870. (Catalogue) Museum of Decorative Arts, Prague 1989, p. 18.
[70] Bazar, 20, 1890 no. 20, p. 153.
[71] Bazar, 23, 1893 no. 10, p. 73.
[72] Bazar, 24, 1893 no. 1, p. 1.
[73] Bazar, 23, 1893 no. 9, p. 41.
[74] Pacina, V., l. c., from p. 78.
[75] Pařížské Mody, 1, 1894 no. 15, p. 313.
[76] Bazar, 27, 1897 no. 12, p. 89.
[77] Bazar , 27, 1897., no. 7, p. 49.
[78] Bazar, 26, 1896 no. 11, pp. 80—81.
[79] Almanach Národní Besedy, l. c., p. 48.
[80] Bazar, 19, 1889 no. 12, p. 89.
[81] Nové Pařížské Mody, 1905 no. 6, p. 1.
[82] Nové Pařížské Mody, 1903 no. 1, p. 1.
[83] Nové Pařížské Mody, 1905 no. 8, p. 1.
[84] Nackrell, A.: Paul Poiret. London 1990, from p. 9.
[85] Vydrová, J., l. c., unpaginated.
[86] Nové Pařížské mody, 1908 no. 19, p. 1.
[87] Dámské módní listy, 7, 1907 no. 5.
[88] Dámské módní listy, 8, 1908 no. 1.
[89] Dámské módní listy, 9, 1909 no. 1.
[90] Vondráčková, J.: Artěl. Tvar 18, 1968, pp. 65—89, Brožová, J.: Artěl — mezník ve vývoji českého užitého umění. Umění a řemesla, 1967, pp. 202—208.
[91] Nové Pařížské Mody, 27, 1914, no. 1, p. 2, no. 2, p. 11.
[92] Nové Pařížské Mody, 27, 1914, no. 1, p. 12.
[93] Český svět, 12, 1915, no. 7 (October 22), unpaginated; no. 12 (November 26); 1916, no. 20 (January 21); 1915, no. 3 (September 24); 1916, no. 24 (February 18), unpaginated.
[94] Nové Pařížské Mody, 27, October 1915, no. 8, pp. 1—3.
[95] Nové Pařížské mody, 27, 114, no.1, p. 10.
[96] Čapek-Chod, K.M.: Jindrové. Praha 1987, pp. 117-118, p. 113.
[97] Nové Pařížské Mody, 27, 1914, no. 3 (November), p. 3, České Mody, 1915 (January), p. 11.
[98] Nové Mody, 28, 1916, no. 20 (July), p. 1.
[99] Dříza, A.: Svéráz a jeho povaha z hlediska českosti. Práce, supplement of Ženské listy, December 15, 1915, p. 1.
[100] Yvonna (Fastrová Olga): Válka — a sukně. Dámské besedy. Supplement of Nové Pařížské Mody, 27, no. 9, p. 4.
[101] Dyk, Al.: Zádruha. In: Svéráz český. Vzorník Zádruhy, 1, no. 1, pp. 4—7, Prague 1916.
[102] Tillnerová, R.: Moda. Ženské listy 1914, no. 1 (January 1), p. 6.
[103] Among pieces awarded with prizes were designs for ladies' dresses by M. Suchardová, L. Fišerová, and P. Jirotková, designs for children's clothes by M. Suchardová, Ž. Felbrová, P. Jirotková, and professor Bouda executed by A. Boudová. Prizes for drawn designs were awarded to M. Květchová, E. Jenšovská, Z. Čechová-Liebscherová. Dámské besedy. Supplement of Nové Pařížské Mody, 27, no. 17 (June 1, 1915).
[104] "Ženské listy" and its supplement "Práce" regularly paid attention to the establishment and development of the national patriotic movement in fashion from no. 4 (March 15, 1915) until 1918. These magazines, similar to "České Mody" from December 1915, also published designs of dresses of national character. For further information and photographs viz. Dámské besedy. July 1, 1915, and catalogues of the abovementioned exhibitions. Also viz. Kybalová, L.: O hnutí svérázovém, Umění a řemesla 1989, no. 2, pp. 60—64.
[105] Nové Mody, 28, 1916, no. 17 (June 7), p. 10; Ženské listy, 1917, no. 9 (August 15), p. 1.
[106] Pávek, M.: Textilní výroba v historickém přehledu I, pp. 170, 205; D.: Náhražky pro textilní průmysl. In: Svéráz český. Vzorník Zádruhy, 2, p. 11, Prague 1916.
[107] Moda. Ženské listy, 1917, no. 10 (September 15), p. 1.
[108] Tillnerová, R.: Z oboru mody. Ženské listy, 1916, no. 6 (May 15), p. 1.
[109] Information contained in autobiography of Helena Mautner-Roubíčková, published under a title "Hella" by American Financial Printers, Washington, USA 1996.

[110]/ Podolský, V.: Královna naší módy. Večerní Praha, October 11, 1991, Český svět, December 24, 1915, unpaginated.
[111]/ Adresář král. hl. m. Prahy a obcí sousedních. Praha 1907, p. 920. Adresář král. hl. m. Prahy a obcí sousedních. Praha 1910, volume II, pp. 141, 172.
[112]/ Epsteinová, H.: Odkud byla. Manuscript in print.
[113]/ Katalog der Ausstelung von Textilarbeiten ausgeführt in den Kunstwerkstätten Marie Teinitzer, Prague 1916, cat. no. 28 (Kleid aus handgewebtem Stoffe mit gefärbten Gürtel. Genäht von Frau Weigert.)
[114]/ The first part of the chapter about men's fashion is a revised and enlarged version of the essay "Tailor's Workshops in Prague in the 19th Century" written by Milena Zeminová, which appeared in the first edition of this publication.
[115]/ Moravcová, M.: Národní oděv roku 1848. /Ke vzniku národně politického symbolu/. Academia, Prague 1986, plates I, XII.
[116]/ Ivanov, M.: Požár Národního divadla aneb příliš mnoho náhod. Prague 1983, p. 40.
[117]/ Zlaté dno, 1, 1862, no. 4, unpaginated.
[118]/ Europäische Modezeitung, 1855, no. 7; Gruber, J.: Obchodní a živnostenská komora v Praze v prvním půlstoletí svého trvání 1850—1900. Praha 1900, pp. 8, 56.
[119]/ Robert Krach, born on March 4, 1818, died on January 17, 1868. AMP, register of citizens — Pražané 1830—1910.
[120]/ Mottl, V.: Umění přistřihačské. Theoretický a praktický návod ku braní míry a přistřihování veškerého oděvu pro pány i dítky, dámských žaketů, livrejí, uniforem pro vojsko, úředníky i dvorní hodnostáře. Bibliotéka řemeslnická. Second, enlarged edition. Prague 1897.
[121]/ 40 let pilné práce "První akademie krejčovské" v Praze. Akademické Modní Listy 38, spring 1934, no. 150, p. 2.
[122]/ Evropské Mody, 10, 1891, no. 6.
[123]/ Jubilejní výstava obvodu Obchodní a živnostenské komory v Praze 1908, Ústřední skupinový katalog no. 1, Prague 1908, pp. 17—19, 313—315.
[124]/ Ibid., pp. 297—300, 310.
[125]/ Ibid., p. 321.
[126]/ Benda, J.: l. c., pp. 33—37, 71—79.
[127]/ Zlaté dno, 9, 1870, no. 5, unpaginated.
[128]/ Uchalová, E.: l.c., p. 50.
[129]/ Zlaté dno, 8, 1869, no. 1, unpaginated.
[130]/ Zlaté dno, 7, 1868, no. 4, unpaginated.
[131]/ Elegantní kroj. Modní list pro pány, 1, 1899, no. 11.
[132]/ Elegantní kroj, 1, 1899, no. 1, p. 2.
[133]/ Elegantní kroj, 4, 1902, no. 9, p. 1.
[134]/ Elegantní svět. Revue pro krásu a chic, 1, 1913, no. 3, p. 7.
[135]/ Elegantní kroj, 2, 1900, no. 3, p. 3, etc., 1902, no. 11, p. 3.
[136]/ Elegantní svět, 1, 1913, no. 1, p. 2 etc.

Choice of literature

Boehn, M. von: Die Mode. Menschen und Moden im neunzehnten Jahrhundert. 1870—1914. Munich 1919.
Buck, A.: Victorian Costume and Costume Accessories. London 1961.
Kybalová, L. — Herbenová, O. — Lamarová, M.: Obrazová encyklopedie módy. Prague 1973.
Bradfield, N.: Costume in Detail. Women's Dress 1730—1930. London 1975.
Robinson, J.: The Golden Age of Style. New York — London 1976.
Thiel, E.: Geschichte des Kostüms. Berlin 1980.
Bond, D.: The Guiness Guide to 20th Century Fashion. London 1981.
Urban, O.: Česká společnost. Prague 1982.
Jílková, J.: Soupis textilních časopisů a ročenek v českých zemích v letech 1787—1982. In: Z dějin textilu. Studie a materiály. vol. 4. Ústí nad Orlicí 1983.
Buxbaum, G.: Mode aus Wien. Vienna 1986.
Kroutvor, J.: Fenomén 1910. Umění a řemesla 1987, no. 4, pp. 23—32.
Zubercová, M.: Tisícročie módy. Bratislava 1988.
Nová encyklopedie českého výtvarného umění. Prague 1995.

Catalogues

Brožová, J.: Historismus. Umělecké řemeslo 1860—1900. UPM, Prague 1975.
Vydrová, J.: Žena doby secese. UPM, Prague 1980.
Rothstein, N.: Four Hundred Years of Fashion. Victoria and Albert Museum, London 1984.
Die Frau im Korsett. Wiener Frauenalltag zwischen Klischee und Wirklichkeit. 1848—1920. Historisches Museum der Stadt Wien. Vienna 1984.
Völker, A.: Wiener Mode + Modefotografie. Die Modeabteilung der Wiener Werkstätte 1911—1932. Katalog des öMAK, Wien. Munich — Paris 1984.
Tarrant, N.: Great Grandmother's Clothes. Women's Fashion in the 1880's. The National Museum of Scotland, Edinburgh 1986.
Drüber und Drunter. Wiener Damenmode von 1900—1914. Historisches Museum der Stadt Wien. Vienna 1987.
Femmes Fin de Siècle 1885—1895. Musée de la Mode et du Costume. Palais Galliera, Paris 1990.
Karner, R.: Wiener Damenmode im Fin de Siècle. Modeammlung des historischen Museums der Stadt Wien, Wien 12, Hetzendorf, Vienna 1995.

A Big Bank from a Small Country

David, Michelangelo, Florence

The Czech economy is on the rise:
experiencing a renaissance of industry
and banking.
And in a renaissance:
those who think small stay small.
The country's largest companies entrust ČSOB
with the managment of their financial assets
and investments.
We also represent the majority of foreign
investors in both Czech and Slovak markets.
We could represent you too.

ČESKOSLOVENSKÁ OBCHODNÍ BANKA, A.S.

Prague   Bratislava   Frankfurt am Main   Chicago   London   Moscow   Paris

Head office: Na Příkopě 14, 115 20 Praha 1, tel.: 02/24 11 11 11, fax: 02/24 22 50 49

Eva Uchalová

Photography: Miloslav Šebek and archives of the Museum of Decorative Arts / Typography: Clara Istlerová / Published by Olympia a.s., Klimentská 1, Prague 1, in cooperation with the Museum of Decorative Arts in Prague in 1997 as its 2867th publication. / First print in Olympia a.s., 128 pages / Editor: Marie Průšová / Technical editor: Jan Zoul / English translation: Capricorn Promotions / Printed by Svoboda a. s., Sazečská 8, Praha 10 / Tem. sk. 02 / 27-41-97

Návod k braní míry a přistřihování,

snímání střihů ze střihových archů „Bazaru"
a zároveň jak se střihy dají zmenšovat neb zvětšovat.

V příloze této je obsaženo:

1. Návod, jak se mohou snímat střihy ze střihových archů.
2. O braní míry.
3. Návod, jak lze zmenšovat neb zvětšovat střihy.
4. O přistřihování.
5. Návod k zhotovování životu a sukně atd.

Návod k zhotovování šatů a braní míry, dále ku shotovování ostatních předmětů do oboru šatstva náležejících, jakož i pokynutí k snímání střihů, zmenšování a zvětšování jejich, jež nalézáme v „Bazaru", poskytne dámám, jež jsou i méně s oborem tím obeznámy, příležitost, že se snadno a za krátký čas vpraví do tajemství praktického krejčování vůbec. Za tou příčinou domníváme se, že není ani třeba dotýkati, jakého prospěchu tedy poskytuje odebírání českého „Bazaru", každé domácnosti, kdež se za rok mnoho peněz dalo vydělat. Střihy podané v arších střihových „Bazaru" jsou shotoveny na průměrně velké čili prostředné tělo dle obyčejné míry; protož nemohou vždy vyhověti každému místu; aby však mohla upotřebit každá našich odběratelek střihů podaných, nutno, povšimnouti si návodu k přistřihování a zmenšování střihů, jakož i způsobu braní míry a snímání střihu dle míry, což při shotovování šatů vůbec věcí jest nejpředností. Zvětšováním neb zmenšováním se střih podaný změní; ale původní jeho forma se přece zachovat, aby ale dobře padl.

1. Návod, jak se mohou snímat střihy ze střihových archů.

a) Aby bylo každé dámě možná dle vzdor četným na střihovém archu se nalézajícím střihům, jejichžto čáry se hojně křižují, v jednotlivých střizích, užívá se k naznačení jednotlivých částí střihů vždy jiných značek, na př. puntíků, čárek, hvězdiček atd. Značky ku každému střihu náležející jsou k vysvětlení vždy udány a proto není věcí tak nesnadnou, vynalezti tu neb onu část střihu na archu.

b) Aby se nezničily vystřihováním jednotlivých střihů z archu všechny ostatní střihy, musejí se střihy z archu pouze snímat, čehož se dá snadno průhledným papírem neb organdinem docíliti. Papír neb organdín se na arch položí a červenou tužkou se střih na vrchu nakreslí a pak dle obrysů vystřihne. Též snímací kolečko k tomu účelu dobře poslouží.

c) Takové části střihů, které se nevejdou pro svou velikost v úplném rozložení na arch, přehnou se a přehnuté části jsou tenkými prolámanými čárkami naznamenány zrovna tak, jak u dílů, jež jsou jen s polovičky nakresleny, na př. rukáv, zadek a t. d., kdež je též čárka, která znamená prostředek, tenkými prolámanými čárkami naznačena. Takové poloviěky jsou vždy doslovně v návodech podotknuty. Nejlépe je, pak-li že se střihnou jednotlivé ohnuté části u dílu střihu vždy o sobě a u kraje, kdež je prolámaná čára, se kousek přidá. Tímto přidaným kouskem se pak přilepí ohnutá část k hlavní části střihu. Prolámanou čárku, která znamená přehyb, není třeba při snímání střihu nakreslit, anať při shotovování věci nemá pražádné platnosti. Střihové části, kdež je dvě neb tré ohnutých částí, jsou vypodobněny obyčejně na střihovém archu v celosti; ale šestnáctkrát zmenšené. Děje se to proto, aby se nemohla ta která dáma, ježto střih chce vystřihnout, při sesazování mýlit. Velmi velké střihy se obyčejně kreslí ve dvou polovičkách na střihový archy a musejí se sesadit tam, kde jsou čárky průměrné stejnými písmeny k sesazování naznamenány, též takové střihy jsou vypodobněny obyčejně šestnáctkrát zmenšené a v celosti, aby bylo vidět, jak se mají sesadit.

d) Nikde není při střizích vpočítáno na založení aneb na švy; musí se tedy vždy při přistřihování k zakládání a na švy přidat.

e) U dílů, jež se podávají pouze s polovičce, jest čárka, která znamená prostřed dílu, tence prolámána as takto (- - - - -). Na tomto místě musí látka ležet vždy v přehybu, aby kus byl dvojitě kladen, dle střihu pak vystřihnut a pak v prostředku úplně v celosti. Kde musí látka v místě tom býti šikmo po niti, je vždy v návodu neb vysvětlení zmínka o tom.

f) Takové díly střihu, které pro délku nemohou býti nakresleny úplně na arch střihový na př. košile, pláště a tak dále, jsou místa, kdež se u přistřihování musí věc dle potřeby sdělšit, naznamenána šipkou.

2. O braní míry.
(K tomu vyobrazení čís. 53. a 54.)

K braní míry třeba setinoměru (centimétre). Čísla míry znamenají se na kousek papíru aneb do malé k tomu určené tobolky a jmeno osoby se k tomu připíše. Objemy se vždy naznamenají pouze s polovice na př. kolem těla, kolem ruky, kolem krku; vždy jen poloviěku oné části střihu jsou též jen s polovice podány a jen polovička se vyměřuje. Délky se berou a naznamenávají úplně.

Při braní míry začne se mírou nahoře kolem těla. Míra položí se na zadek přes šířku, táhne se pod pážím až napřed se v prostřed prsou spojí. Míra nesmí se položit ani tuze volně, ani tuze těsně. Míra naznamená se jen s polovičky. Dole kolem pásu se položí setinoměr něco těsněji, aneb tak, jak si kdo šaty přeje, buď těsněji neb volněji. Polovička objemu se napíše.

Délka životu měří se pod pážím až k boku. Šířka přes prsa měří se od jednoho průramku k druhému zrovna přes prsa, jak na vyobrazení č. 50. naznamenáno. Míra nechá se dosti volně.

Míra zadku do délky, šířky a délka na ramenou béře se dle jasného vyobrazení č. 54. Délka rukávu béře se na vnitřní straně ramene od průramku pod pážím až dolů k ohybu. (Viz vyobrazení č. 53.)

Délka sukně se béře napřed od prostředku pasu až dolů a ve stranách taktéž. Chceme-li shotoviti přiléhající paletko neb kazajku atd., musí se bráti míra, jako na život jen v šířce o něco volnější. Aby bylo paletko dosti dlouhé, třeba též vzíti míru délky životu pod pážím. U volného paletka béře se pouze míra šířky přes prsa, zadek a délka na ramenou.

Č. 53. Zmenšování a zvětšování střihů a vyměřování střihů dle míry.

3. Návod, jak lze zvětšovat a zmenšovat střihy.
K tomu vyobr. č. 55.

Naznamenanou míru, kterou jsme vzali na jakémsi těle, porovnáme se střihem aneb lépe řečeno, vyměříme dle ní střih. Míra se k tomu účelu položí na střih, jak **fig. 1.** až 3. na vyobrazení čís. 55. naznačuje. (Přednice, stranní díl a polovička zadku k životu.) Nedá-li se užit střihu dle míry, musí se střih

Č. 53. Braní míry. Pohled s předu. (K tomu vyobr. č. 54.)

Č. 54. Braní míry. Pohled se zadu. (K tomu vyobr. č. 53.)